By the Editors of CONSUMER GUIDE®

The Complete Guide To
Building A Better Body

Library of Congress Cataloging in Publication Data
Main entry under title:
Complete guide to building a better body.

    1. Bodybuilding.   I. Consumer guide.
GV514.C65   1978   646.7'5   78-20432
ISBN 0-517-27464-7

This edition published by:
Beekman House
A Division of Crown Publishers, Inc.
One Park Avenue
New York, N.Y. 10016
By arrangement with Publications International, Ltd.

Cover Design: Frank E. Peiler
Cover Photos: Courtesy of Weider Health and Fitness
                 and Betty Weider
Illustrations: Steven Boswick

Manufactured in the United States of America
    2   3   4   5   6   7   8   9 10

Contents

Dreaming about a better body won't do; you have to build the body you want in a safe and sensible manner. Embark upon the CONSUMER GUIDE® program and you can develop the body of your dreams — firmer, stronger, and more powerful.

What A Better Body Means To You

YEARS AGO, most people took physical attributes — hair color, eye color, height, and weight — for granted. The way you were born was the way you stayed, like it or not. Today, however, many people go to great lengths to change their appearance; hair can be dyed, contact lenses can hide the natural color of the eyes, high-heeled shoes can temporarily elevate height, and diets can cause weight loss or gain.

Of all the physical changes that men and women perform on their bodies, though, the most beneficial — and

Is your body all it could be? Take a good look in the mirror.

perhaps the most satisfying — are those which promote good health and good shape. Today, better bodies are built, not born.

Do you need or want a program to build a better body? The answer to that question can be read in the mirror.

Stand in front of your mirror. Gaze into it, and be honest with yourself. Are you totally pleased with the body you see there?

If the answer to that question is not a firm "yes," don't despair. Take heart. First of all, you are not alone. Second, and most important, there is a great deal you can do to change that body for the better.

Bodies can be toned — that is, they can be reshaped into attractive proportions. Sags can be firmed up, soft flesh made solid, and ugly bulges turned into attractive muscle. Body toning need not lead to the rippled, over-developed appearance of Arnold Schwarzenegger; rather, it will result in the lean, smooth, and firm bodies every man and woman desires. It can even replace the pipestem limbs and tubular torsos that bedevil the skinny with well-shaped flesh and muscle.

Almost anyone can improve the shape of his or her body. How? Probably the most efficient way to do it is by working with weights.

Weight training was at one time considered a masculine sport and exercise. Today we know much better: body building can benefit both sexes. Today many beauty queen contestants work out with weights; so do models and movie actresses. Men's and women's bodies respond differently to weight training, allowing the two sexes to achieve quite different results from the same activity.

Natural, healthy development — that is really the principal reason for building a better body. But it is far from being the only reason. There are a host of side benefits as well. Improved strength and power, better muscular endurance, a healthier mental attitude — all contribute to the way you are able to handle your daily activities. When you work around the house, in the yard, or at your job, you will find that you are doing so with less effort and strain than before. In many cases, you will find that the results of your work are more satisfying, too.

Weight training is practical, too. Clyde Emrich, a former Olympic weight lifter and presently strength and fitness coordinator for the Chicago Bears professional football team, talks about the all-around utility of body building. "You don't just use weight training if you want to be a football player or a wrestler," he says. "You use it to help improve your tennis game, your golf game, or anything else that requires basic bodily strength. You will be better at any physical activity if the muscles you use for the activity are stronger and capable of better endurance."

The benefits of weight training are within the reach of just about everyone. For this reason the Editors and consultants of CONSUMER GUIDE® have put together a basic program designed to help you build a better body. We have developed the program in such a way that you can automatically tailor it to your own needs, physical characteristics, and personal goals. Starting out at the appropriate level (depending on your sex, age, and physical condition), you can proceed upward, step by step, until the body you see in the mirror comes to resemble the body you've always wanted.

Weight Training And You

WE ENTER the world with a nearly perfect, though immature, body. This body is a marvelous machine, constructed of blood and brain and bone and sinew and muscle, including that most fantastic muscle of all, the heart. Unfortunately, in the process of growing up, too many of us fail to maintain the machine as well as we should.

Our modern, mechanized world is a thief. It robs us of exercise. Everything around us invites us to take it easy, to let technological devices mow the lawn and wash the car; we ride on wheels rather than walk, sit in swivel chairs, play games on an electronic screen rather than on a playing field. In other words, we live a life that requires little or no physical effort. Of course, we reap the results of such inactivity: shrunken muscles, weakened organs, obesity, lazy bowels, mental depression, anxiety, and a host of other weaknesses and ailments.

What can we do about it? First, remember that it's your body and yours alone. As sole proprietor and lifetime tenant of that body, you are the person totally in charge of it. Nobody else can change your body for you. Only you can do it. You can make the decision to let it slide downhill. Or you can make the decision to embark on a program of improving your body, both in appearance and physical functioning. A well-planned, regularly maintained, satisfying lifetime system of development and maintenance is within your grasp.

Dreaming about building a better body, however, or saying to yourself, "I really ought to do something about it sometime," won't strengthen a single muscle or pump an ounce of oxygenated blood through your arteries. The opposite of dreaming is doing. We recommend you do it by working with weight-training equipment in a carefully planned program designed precisely for you and your needs.

The idea of working out with barbells and dumbbells has been misunderstood by many people for a long time. Here are some of the most common myths associated with the activity.

Weight training will make you muscle-bound.

It will not. A muscle-bound person is one whose muscles are enlarged and less elastic. Occasionally some weight lifters who do not follow proper training principles become muscle-bound, but you needn't fear that. With basic weight training you will simply firm up and strengthen your muscles without any adverse effect on elasticity, agility, or general body flexibility.

Weight training will make a woman masculine.

Not at all. Women will not develop masculine-type muscles or a masculine shape. They will maintain and even enhance their natural female shape.

Muscles will turn to fat as soon as you stop active lifting.

They will not; muscles are muscles and fat is fat. One will not change into the other. You can, however, reduce the volume of fat and increase the volume of muscle in your body if you take minimal efforts to keep yourself in relatively good physical shape.

Weight training is a young person's sport.

Age is no restriction. Many elderly people work out regularly with weights. And some of the most dramatic results can be achieved by the middle-aged body builder.

Weight training involves the lifting of extremely heavy weights.
No. That is power lifting, a separate sport. Proper weight training involves lifting weights no heavier than you are comfortable with.

Your Body And The CONSUMER GUIDE® Program

REMEMBER the beach bully kicking sand in the weakling's face in all those ads for the Charles Atlas body building programs during the 1940s and 1950s? Over the years, a host of similar programs — all claiming to make a person stronger and more Adonis-like — have come and gone, leaving in their wake thousands of disillusioned individuals. None of these programs met individual needs. None enabled the person taking up the exercise to create his or her own program; they all assumed that what was good for one person was appropriate for everyone else as well.

The CONSUMER GUIDE® program is totally different. Tailored to the individual, it can be personalized for age, sex, and physical condition.

This program — carefully designed for people who want a better looking, well-proportioned, and stronger body — is aimed simply at providing an individualized course of body toning, body conditioning, strength development and muscle endurance. It is a weight-lifting program, planned so that you can adjust your efforts to meet your goals.

Because this is a body toning program and not a complete physical fitness program, *we strongly advocate that you supplement this program with a good program of cardiovascular exercise: e.g., running, walking, or other sustained efforts that will build and strengthen the heart and lungs.* The long-term effect of sedentary life on the heart, the blood vessels, and the respiratory system is damaging; it can even shorten your life. Understand that body-building activities cannot substitute for cardiovascular exercise, but when coupled with a cardiovascular exercise program the CONSUMER GUIDE® program presented in this book should help reverse any physical decline and guide you on a course to developing and maintaining a fully fit body.

Toning Your Body

BODY TONING is one of the most noticeable benefits you can achieve by following the CONSUMER GUIDE® program. "Tone" is appearance — that condition in which all the muscles are naturally well-shaped and visually appealing. Body organs and tissues should be firm. In other words, body tone means no flab!

"I feel great!" is the typical reaction of people who have been on a weight-training program for a few weeks. They feel great because they look good. A body with tone is a body in harmony with itself. It can do what it is supposed to do — like a well-tuned Stradivarius violin or a beautifully tuned engine in a racing car.

You will probably not be able to sense the particular muscles or organs that are making you feel so good; they will all be working together smoothly. With a regular routine of weight training, your body — that tremendously complex and responsive natural machine that you were born with — will achieve its proper tone. And it will make you feel great!

What happens to our bodies when we do not exercise them? Those nearly perfect, youthful bodies begin to develop fat places, skinny places, sags, and bulges. Persons of both sexes stop growing at both ends but often continue to grow in the middle, especially if they happen to have sit-down-behind-a-desk jobs. Some men and women develop a pot belly; others hunch and stoop, especially if they are tall. And women find themselves with less-than-firm busts and experiencing a general feeling of flabbiness. Both sexes often develop bad habits of slouching, duck walking, wobbling, and teetering off balance, as well as simply having weight in the wrong places.

Fortunately, all these appearance defects can be remedied. A few simple exercises, conducted vigorously and routinely, can lead you toward a freshly refurbished body. Remember, though, if you are to have a better body, you must be the one who builds it.

Posture And Carriage

IN ADDITION to body tone, you can achieve better body posture through the CONSUMER GUIDE® program.

Have you ever arrived early at a party or a meeting and simply watched the people as they come in? Some of them slump in, some sort of slide in, some send in their stomachs first, some jerk their way in, some totter in, and some waddle in. Some plod in with an artificial, frozen gait; some march in like toy soldiers; and others come in shyly or hesitantly, as though they might panic and run if somebody sneezed.

Not everyone enters a room this way, though. Some people walk in with a posture and bearing that says to all present: Here is somebody special. This somebody special doesn't have to be a very big person, or beautiful, or handsome, or well-dressed. No, these special people stand out from the crowd because of the way they carry themselves. Their posture breathes self-confidence, composure, and grace.

Good posture and carriage do not come naturally to most of us. We have to work to attain it. Some of us have it when we are young but lose it as we grow older. Cultivating good posture and carriage (or regaining it) is important to good appearance, but it is important in other ways as well. Once you have trained the muscles that enable you to stand, walk, and sit properly, you place less strain on these muscles, have fewer back problems, and suffer less fatigue. Good carriage can make you not only an attractive and impressive person, but also a tireless walker and a good jogger. In short, good carriage can increase your overall vitality — one of the many dividends derived from a well-balanced body.

Weight Control

IF YOUR SOLE objective is to lose weight, you are involving yourself with the wrong program. Concentrate instead on dieting and on increasing your level of activity.

The CONSUMER GUIDE® body-building program is dedicated to shaping and toning your body. Follow it and

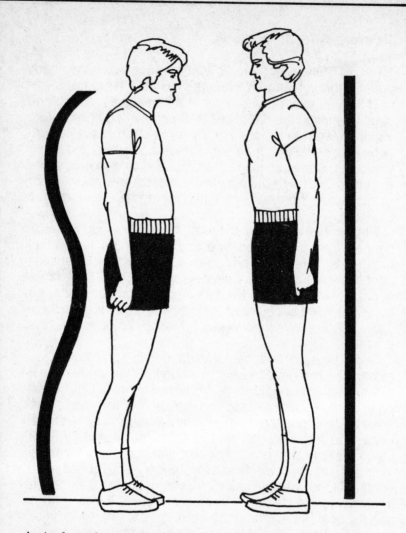

Lack of muscle tone often shows up as poor posture. Build a better body and your posture will improve as well.

you will tone the muscles of your body and look much better. But you will not necessarily lose weight, especially at the beginning stages. In fact, if you are truly obese you may end up gaining weight at the outset because you will be building stronger muscles. Quite simply, muscle is denser than fat and is therefore heavier.

Anyone who is obese — that is, has a good amount of flab — would be wise to try to take off and control his or her fat before starting a body-building program. Adding some weight when you are already too heavy can be very self-defeating. If weight or fat is a problem and yet you want to get started with the CONSUMER GUIDE® program, be sure to supplement your body toning efforts with proper dieting and some aerobic exercise.

As you proceed in the CONSUMER GUIDE® program, you will discover some very interesting factors contributing to body weight control. For example, a person with well-toned muscles will burn off more calories for any given activity than will a person whose body composition is fatty rather than muscular.

Body building can also aid in weight control by decreasing appetite. If you conduct your regimen of exercise — body-building and cardiovascular activities — shortly before mealtimes, you will find yourself eating less. Good exercise (not labor or extreme exercise, however) tends to make you eat less food when you sit down at the table.

Building Strength

HAVE YOU ever felt short of breath or full of pain when suddenly called upon to lift an automobile tire, a stereo set, a bag of groceries, or some other reasonably heavy load? And how do your legs feel when you walk up two flights of stairs? How about your arms when you are painting a ceiling or wall?

Muscular strength can be deceptive. Take the case of George, for example. Proud of his prowess as a golfer, George could be found on the golf course at least every Saturday and Sunday. He bragged about what great physical shape he was in, until one day his wife — a devoted gardener — asked him to help her transplant some honeysuckle bushes to a better location. After a brief bout with a shovel George gave up in exhaustion. His wife was left to complete the digging while he took two aspirin and settled down in front of the TV set.

George simply did not have the muscular strength to perform the routine gardening tasks that appeared so simple. His wife was stronger in this respect, not only because she regularly handled the full range of chores in the garden, but also because she had been working out with weights and had trained herself to lift without back stress.

Then there's Judy, who rode her bicycle faithfully in an effort to keep her body trim. She pedaled from two to four miles a day. In bad weather she pedaled the stationary bike she had set up in the family room, adjusting the tension on the drag wheel to give her muscles plenty of action.

While bicycling, Judy kept her fingers clasped around the handlebars; in other words, her fingers and forearm muscles did not share in the power and flexibility being developed in her leg muscles. As a consequence, when the time came to get dinner ready, Judy had to ask her strong-fingered, 15-year-old son to open a jar of olives.

Body building will not turn George into a circus strongman who can bend steel bars, nor will it strengthen Judy into a Wonder Woman. But a regularly maintained program of weight training will strengthen all your muscles. You will then be able to confidently perform any special task you encounter in work or play.

Muscle Endurance

BUILDING muscular endurance is a somewhat different process from building muscular strength. The same efforts and exercises you would use for body toning are used for building muscular endurance, but they contribute to a totally separate muscle quality. Muscle endurance means you are able to use muscles for an extended period of time.

Many kinds of ordinary physical activities require muscular endurance. Concert piano playing requires it. So does mountain climbing. The bricklayer who works all day at his trade needs muscular endurance. The long distance bicycle rider or cross-country skier needs this quality — and plenty of it! Soccer, football, basketball, and baseball players depend on their muscular endurance to stay in the game. Likewise, the person working around the house or in the garden benefits from improved muscle endurance. The common thread that runs through all these activities is that they are extended efforts. If you do not have adequate muscle endurance, you will not be able to complete them — and that can be a problem if they are efforts you should and want to be able to finish.

Many people never think of a singer as an athlete. Yet singers are often called upon to exert a remarkable amount of muscular endurance. The great Italian opera tenor Luciano Pavarotti once consented to telecast a two-hour solo concert from the Metropolitan Opera House. Even seasoned singers were aghast. "How could he get through it?" they asked. They knew that an operatic singer has to have great power. In the regular business of singing operas, however, singers get many rest periods between the taxing arias that they must perform. In this performance, there would be no rest periods.

Pavarotti sang beautifully throughout the entire two hours, and he sang some of the most difficult pieces in the operatic repertoire. The television audience could tell that he was perspiring a lot, but so what? Great athletes perspire when they are pushing themselves to the limits of endurance.

At the end, Pavarotti was singing as easily and with as much delicacy and grace as he had at the beginning. What carried him through? The tremendous muscular endurance of his diaphragm, chest, and other muscles that he used for singing. He had trained them for endurance, and they did not let him down. It was not only a great musical performance, but — in its own way — a tremendous athletic performance as well.

The person who can put forth an amazing burst of strength for an instant often has no staying power because of his or her lack of muscular endurance. The CONSUMER GUIDE® program is designed to help you achieve muscular endurance for both the routine and the unexpected tasks you may be called upon to perform. And you will be achieving this muscular endurance at the same time that you are toning your body.

Increasing Physical Power

POWER. It is yours with the CONSUMER GUIDE® body-building program. But this is not the power of a Superman

Power (a combination of strength, speed, and flexibility) is an important factor in playing most sports well. You can make yourself more powerful through a good body-building program.

or a Wonder Woman. Power, as we define it, is a combination of strength, speed, and flexibility. It is rewarding to be able to perform the tasks that a strong person can perform, but it is not very helpful if at the same time you are slow-moving and lacking in agility. There are many situations in which you need to be able to move fast and flexibly, while at the same time you are acting with strength.

Sailing a boat is a situation demanding this kind of power. Playing good tennis is another. Driving a car, either in competition or on a congested highway, can be another. In baseball, the center fielder who makes a spectacular one-handed catch of a fly ball and fires the ball back to the infield provides an outstanding example of speed, flexibility and strength (plus accuracy). This is power in action. Such power can be yours when you start to build a better body.

Other Health Benefits

MANY OTHER health benefits can be yours when you follow a good body-building program. First of all, you will simply begin to feel better. If you are like most people, you suffer mysterious and annoying aches and cramps, and you wonder where they all came from. These troublesome pains will often disappear when you regularly work at building and maintaining your body. You will become better able to enjoy your work and your play. You won't have to beg off when the boss asks you to take on a special assignment or when a friend suggests jogging with him or playing a couple of sets of tennis.

You will normally find that you are becoming a friendlier, happier, and more considerate sort of person. At work, you may get along better with other people and not feel the urge to blow your top over problems. At home, your family may find that you have made a great change for the better.

There are several reasons for all these changes. When you look good, your self-esteem is increased. And when that happens you feel well and are easier to get along with. Body-building exercises, moreover, have a way of reducing the effects of stress and tension; the exercises contribute to a healthier mental state and attitude.

One very distinct physical benefit of the CONSUMER GUIDE® body-building program is the alleviation of varicose veins. Obese people (with large abdomens) and pregnant women are especially susceptible to varicose veins in the legs. Abdominal pressure is exerted on the large veins in the legs. This pressure, in turn restricts the blood flow and causes the valves in the veins to function improperly. Blood can pool and push the veins toward the body surface, causing the unsightly condition we call varicose veins.

Body-building exercises that strengthen the abdomen will help prevent this pressure from being exerted on leg veins. Body-toning exercises for the legs also contribute to maintaining these veins in their proper place.

Building a better body is not a panacea for your aches, pains, and ailments. But it can make a large contribution to your physical and mental well-being. A regular program of weight training can make your body look better, feel better, and be stronger. In effect, such a program fashions your body into one you will be proud of — a pretty substantial package of benefits by anyone's standards.

Basically healthy and truly
sincere in your desire to
shape yourself up? If so, then
now's the time to get started
in a body-building program
specially designed to meet
your needs and accomplish
your goals.

Getting Started

BODY-BUILDING exercises can be divided into two types — isotonic and isometric. Both terms come from the Greek, the "iso" meaning "equal." In each type of exercise a muscular effort equal to the need is put forth, but the nature of that effort is different depending upon whether the exercise is isometric or isotonic.

Isotonic exercises are those in which an object is raised, lowered, pulled, or pushed through the full range of muscular motion. Weight lifting is isotonic, as are calisthenics. Walking and running are also isotonic, muscular exertion being used to propel the weight of the body. Other isotonic exercise activities include dancing, softball, soccer, basketball, football, and tennis.

Isometric exercises, on the other hand, are those that involve exerting one set of muscles against another set of muscles, or against some type of immovable object. These exercises — which include pushing against a wall, stretching facial muscles, and arm wrestling, differ from isotonics in the way they tone body muscles.

Isometric exercises are, in terms of the CONSUMER GUIDE® program, treated as supplements to body-building efforts. They are discussed and illustrated in the chapter on "Extending The Program."

In order to build a well-toned and well-shaped body, with attractive, strong, and capable muscles, an isotonic exercise program of weight training is best.

Who Should — Who Shouldn't

WHO SHOULD take up a weight-training program such as the one described in this book? The answer is easy: the program can be taken up by anybody who is healthy and has a sincere desire to improve the appearance of his or her body.

Who shouldn't take up the program is perhaps a more crucial question, and one that is not quite as easy to answer. Generally speaking, however, a sustained weight-training program — even a tailored and individualized one such as the one CONSUMER GUIDE® advocates — should not be undertaken by people who have any of the following conditions: heart disease; high blood pressure; hernia; lower back ailments; spinal problems; orthopedic problems; is pregnant; or has not attained the age of puberty.

If any of these conditions applies to you, discuss the possibility of weight lifting with your doctor. It is possible that your doctor may permit you to take up a modified version of the training program. For example, if you have an orthopedic problem like a bad knee, you can probably still perform arm and upper body weight-training exercises. But you should consult your doctor first.

If you have none of these conditions, or are not aware of them, your very first step in getting started should be to have a full physical examination. Have this examination before attempting the CONSUMER GUIDE® program, or any of the fitness tests, warm-up activities, or the alternate exercise program. Only your physician can determine whether you are healthy and fit enough to take part. Since a simple medical exam can avoid many future problems, we heartily recommend it to all potential builders of a better body.

Know Yourself

BEFORE you start any program for building up and toning your body, you really should know a little about that body. If you do, you will be aware of what you can expect from exercising it.

It would certainly simplify the situation if all human beings had similar shapes — all tall and lean or all short and plump. Nature, however, likes variety, and so we have different body types. The three basic body types are referred to as endomorph, mesomorph, and ectomorph. Knowing your body type is important to your body-building activities since different activities can be correlated to different body types in order to get the best results.

The three body types are determined by estimating the relative proportion of fat, muscle, and bone in a body. There are, however, many variations in the physical structure of human beings. The endomorph has a round, soft body, usually with small bones and little muscular development. The weight is centered around the abdomen; arms and legs are rather small, the face round, and the neck short. Pads of fat are found around the backs of the hips, on the abdomen, and on the buttocks and thighs.

The ectomorph has the opposite body type. This person has thin muscles and thin bones. Ectomorphs are often very tall, with long necks, long arms, and long legs but

20

frequently short trunks. Some ectomorphs tend toward rounded shoulders, weak upper arms, and weak thighs. The ectomorph has very little fat on the body and all too often lacks the muscular strength to hold the body up properly. As a consequence, the posture of an ectomorph tends to be poor.

The prefix "meso" means "in the middle." Appropriately, the mesomorph is usually of moderate height, muscular, and big boned. In other words, the mesomorph is between the endomorph and the ectomorph. Mesomorphs have rather hearty appearances — broad shoulders, well-developed chests, slender waists, and broad hips. Mesomorphs usually find it easy to lift and carry heavy objects.

The CONSUMER GUIDE® program can be beneficial to all three body types. You cannot change your body type, but you can do a great deal to perfect the body type with which you were born. For example, a slender, ectomorphic runner such as Frank Shorter will never develop an Arnold Schwarzenegger body, no matter how often or much he works with weights. He will, however, develop a good, strong, muscular body for his body type.

Know What You Want To Achieve

IF YOU ARE obese, you probably want to take the fat off and add some well-shaped muscle. If you are skinny, you probably want to put some weight and muscle on your body. If you are soft and flabby in various areas, you probably want to convert that flab into hard, lean muscle tissue.

Before you embark upon the CONSUMER GUIDE® program, you should determine just what you mean by "a better body." Once you do, you can tailor the program to meet your needs. How do you do that? You start by going back to the mirror.

This time, take off all your clothes and study yourself in a full-length mirror. Look at one body feature at a time and think about it. Can it be improved? Neck? Arms? Chest? Shoulders? Bust? Waist? Abdomen? Buttocks? Legs?

Now consider your posture. Walk toward the mirror, and then away from it (looking over your shoulder). How do you honestly feel you shape up?

Think of your muscles in large units. How about your upper arms? When you make a fist and tense your biceps, do the muscles look good? When you straighten out your arm and feel the muscles at the back of your upper arm, are you satisfied with what you find? What about the forearms?

Look at the muscles of your chest and neck. Are they flabby? Do you have a nice smooth chin? Pinch either side of your waist — do you detect any muscles there? Poke hard into your abdomen; what muscular response do you get? Stand on your tiptoes and examine the muscles of your legs.

Finally, make a mental or written note of your features. Your observations will serve as a guide to individualizing the CONSUMER GUIDE® program to suit your needs and desires.

Preparing Yourself

NEVER START exercising your muscles without first considering the condition of your vital organs — especially the heart and lungs. Physical fitness authorities warn that you can't build muscles unless your internal organs are in good condition. Architects build from the outside in, but body builders should build from the inside out.

If your cardiovascular system is in good shape, it will contribute to your muscular efforts. The respiratory and circulatory systems take in and distribute oxygen, one of the fuels you will need for building muscles.

Have a full physical examination to learn the condition of your cardiovascular system. If it is in good enough shape for you to undertake serious exercise, you can proceed. Your chances for being in good cardiovascular shape, of course, are greatly enhanced if you participate regularly in running, swimming, cycling, or other forms of aerobic activity.

Your doctor may give you a stress ECG as part of your physical exam. If so, he will be able to tell you the level of your present aerobic abilities. If your doctor does not give you a stress ECG, determine your aerobic fitness on your own. There are a number of simple but carefully and professionally developed fitness tests. A bench step test, for example, measures the ability of your body to recover from strenuous exercise. Approach such a test sensibly — exert yourself, but do not push yourself to exhaustion.

The Kasch Pulse Recovery Test

This test, developed by Dr. Fred Kasch, Ph.D., of San Diego State University, requires only:

1. A bench or step exactly twelve inches high (a stack of newspapers securely tied together will work, or two six-inch stair steps).
2. A clock or watch with a sweep second hand.
3. A friend to help you with the counting.

Procedure:

TO BEGIN, step up onto the bench or step, stand fully erect, then step back down from the bench. Do this for three minutes, at the rate of 24 steps per minute. (That's a full step-up-step-down every 2.5 seconds.) Both feet must step onto the bench and return to the floor each time. The action should be even and relaxed, not jumping or hopping: step up on the bench with your right foot, up with your left foot, return your right foot to the floor, and return your left foot to the floor. This completes one cycle.

In the unlikely event that you find the test too vigorous, stop, and rate your fitness level "poor."

When you've done this for 3 minutes, sit down and relax — without talking — for 5 seconds. Then take your pulse rate for 60 seconds.

To get an accurate pulse count, place the middle three fingers of one hand on the underside of the opposite wrist. If you have difficulty locating your pulse there, try placing the same three fingers on either side of your throat just below the joint of the jaw. Count each "push" or "throb" you feel against your fingertips. (Some people need a little practice in finding the pulse; try it once or twice prior to the test.)

To complete the test and determine your fitness level, locate your pulse rate in the following table.

CIRCULO-RESPIRATORY ENDURANCE RATINGS, MEASURED BY PULSE RECOVERY RATE*

| FITNESS | 6-12 yrs. | | 18-26 yrs. | | 33-57 yrs. | |
LEVEL	BOYS	GIRLS	MEN	WOMEN	MEN	WOMEN
Excellent	73-82	81-92	69-75	76-84	63-76	73-86
Good	83-92	93-104	76-83	85-94	77-90	87-100
Average	93-103	105-118	84-92	95-105	91-106	101-117
Fair	104-113	119-130	93-99	106-116	107-120	118-130
Poor	114-123	131-142	100-106	117-127	121-134	131-144

Note: If your age group is not listed, use the figure in the closest age range.

F. W. Kasch, Ph.D., San Diego State University, Exercise Physiology Laboratory, personal communication, 1974.

Obviously, this test is not a substitute for a stress test. But it does give you an idea of where you would fall on an aerobic fitness continuum. The test also allows you to better "prescribe" your exercise dosage.

After testing your cardiovascular condition, you can go on to test your muscular condition. All you need in order to measure your own minimum muscular strength is someone to hold your feet. The series of tests is called the modified Kraus-Weber Test, and scoring consists of a simple pass or fail on each test. A failure to pass any single test is an indication that your strength level is so low that your entire body health may be in danger. Here are the tests:

Modified Kraus-Weber Test

Step 1

Step 2

Modified Kraus-Weber Test

Test 1
(for strength of the abdominal and psoas (loin) muscles).
1. Lie on your back, legs flat, hands clasped behind your neck.
2. With someone holding your legs down, or with your feet hooked under a big chair, perform one sit-up, touching your elbows to your knees.

Modified Kraus-Weber Test

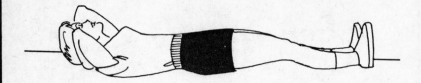

Step 1

Step 2

Test 2
(for strength of the abdominal muscles without the aid of the psoas).
1. Begin in the position used for Test 1.
2. Bend your knees, drawing the heels close to the buttocks.
3. Keeping heels flat on the floor, perform one sit-up.

Modified Kraus-Weber Test

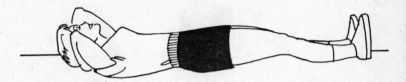

Step 1

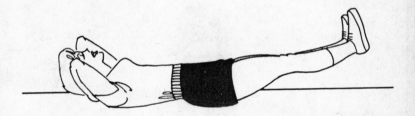

Step 2

Test 3
(for strength of the psoas and lower abdominal muscles).
1. Begin in the position used for Test 1.
2. Lift your legs, knees straight and legs fully extended, until your heels are 10 inches off the floor.
3. Hold this position for 10 seconds.

Modified Kraus-Weber Test

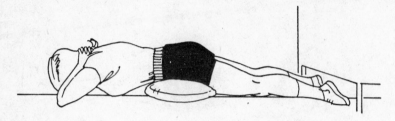

Step 2

Step 3

Test 4
(for strength of the upper back muscles).
1. Lie face down with a pillow under your hips and lower abdomen.
2. Clasp your hands behind your neck. Your feet should be held motionless by a friend or tucked under a heavy chair.
3. Raise your chest, head, and shoulders.
4. Hold them off the floor for 10 seconds.

Modified Kraus-Weber Test

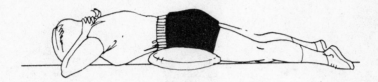

Step 1

Step 2

Test 5
(for strength of the lower back).
1. Begin in the position used for Test 4.
2. Have someone hold your upper-back down. Raise your legs off the floor, keeping your knees straight.
3. Hold this position for 10 seconds.

Modified Kraus-Weber Test

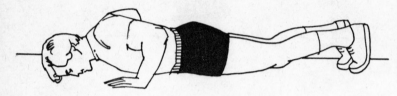

Step 1

Step 2

Test 6
(for push-up strength).
   1. Lie face down on floor with your feet together, elbows
      bent, hands under your shoulders, palms down.
   2. Keep your body straight and push it off the floor by
      straightening your arms.
   3. Return to the starting position.

Muscular endurance, the ability to perform a specific task for a long time without excessive muscular fatigue, is relatively hard to measure because there are so many different muscles and muscle groups to consider. Most experts agree, however, that general muscular endurance is reasonably well represented in the sit-up. YMCA experts have used the sit-up to test muscular endurance for a number of years. Here is the test they offer.

YMCA Sit-Up Test
   1. Lie flat on your back, with your hands on your thighs and your feet slipped under a heavy chair, chest, couch, or bed.
   2. Raise the head, then the shoulders and upper trunk in an upward curl, sliding your hands forward until your fingertips just touch your kneecaps.
   3. Return to the original position, flat on your back.
   4. Do as many sit-ups as possible, to a maximum of 45.

MUSCULAR ENDURANCE RATING MEASURED IN SIT-UPS

Rating	Men	Women
Excellent	50 or more	50 or more
Good	40 - 49	35 - 49
Average	25 - 39	22 - 34
Fair	15 - 24	12 - 21
Poor	14 or fewer	11 or fewer

Preparing Your Muscles

ONCE YOU have determined that you are cardiovascularly and muscularly ready to begin weight training, it's a good idea to ease into such training with some brief sessions devoted to calisthenics. If you practice these calisthenics for a few weeks prior to the actual weight lifting, you will help activate unused muscles and thereby reduce the risk of injury. Such calisthenics are not a prerequisite for the CONSUMER GUIDE® program, but they do help the beginner ease into the program gradually.

Here are some calisthenic exercises designed to get various muscles and muscle groups into better shape.

Calisthenic Exercise

Step 1

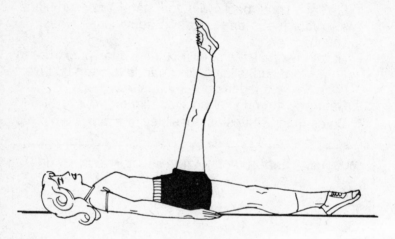

Step 2

Straight Leg Lift
(to strengthen thigh, hip, and abdominal muscles).
1. Lie flat on your back, feet together: arms are at sides, hands with palms down.
2. Raise left leg smoothly until it is perpendicular to the body.
3. Lower it slowly back to the floor.
4. Repeat with other leg.
5. Repeat complete cycle 5 to 10 times: increase gradually number of repetitions.
NOTE: Be certain the lower back is kept on the floor throughout this exercise.

Calisthenic Exercise

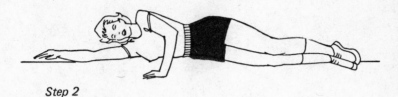

Step 2

Step 3

Side Leg Lift
(to strengthen thigh, hip, and lateral abdominal muscles).
1. Lie on your side with both feet together.
2. Extend bottom arm straight out under your head; use other arm for balancing.
3. Raise upper leg gradually and smoothly until it is approximately two feet above the floor.
4. Return it gradually to the starting position.
5. Repeat 5 to 10 times.
6. Lie on other side and repeat procedure.

Calisthenic Exercise

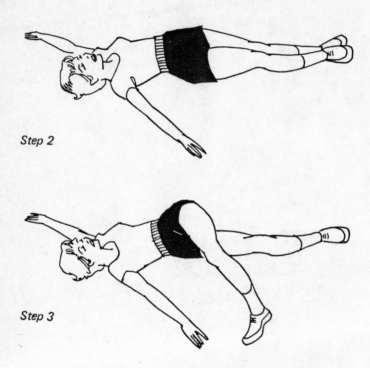

Step 2

Step 3

Leg-Over
(to strengthen hip and thigh muscles).
1. Lie flat on back: feet together.
2. Extend arms straight out perpendicular from body.
3. Raise left leg straight up; roll body to the right, keeping left leg stiff; touch left foot to the floor as close to the opposite hand as possible.
4. Slowly return left leg to the starting position.
5. Repeat with other leg.
6. Repeat cycle 5 times; more if possible.

Calisthenic Exercise

Step 1

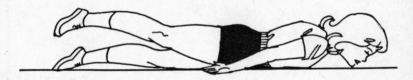

Step 3

The Flutter
(to strengthen thigh, buttocks and back muscles).
1. Lie flat on stomach with arms alongside the body:
   hands with palms up.
2. Keep head and shoulders on the floor.
3. Raise feet and kick in an alternating fashion.
4. Return to starting position.
5. Repeat 5 times.

Calisthenic Exercise

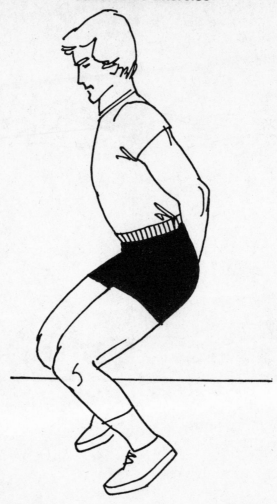

Step 2

Half Knee Bend
(to strengthen the thigh muscles).
1. Stand erect with feet slightly apart and hands on hips or behind back.
2. Bend the knees to a 90-degree angle (the heels are allowed to come off the floor).
3. Return to the starting position.
4. Repeat 10 times.

Calisthenic Exercise

Step 3

Skier's Exercise

(to strengthen the thigh muscles and stretch the calves).
1. Stand erect with feet close together and hands on hips.
2. Bend knees to a 90-degree angle and turn both alternately to the left and right.
3. When the knees are bent to the left, move both arms to the left. When the knees are bent to the right, both arms go to the right.
4. Repeat 10 times on each side.

Calisthenic Exercise

Step 2

Side Stretch
(to firm the thighs, hips, and buttocks).
   1. Stand erect with your hands on your hips, and your feet spread wider apart than shoulder-width.
   2. Lunge to the right, bending the right leg, keeping the left leg extended.
   3. Return to the starting position and repeat to the opposite side.
   4. Repeat sequence 10 times.

Calisthenic Exercise

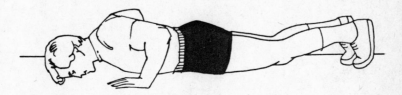

Step 2

Step 3

The Modified Push-Up
(to strengthen arm, shoulder, chest and back muscles).
1. Lie flat on stomach; legs together.
2. Place hands palms down, just outside shoulders.
3. Raise torso and thighs until you are supported by your hands, knees, and lower legs: your arms should be fully straightened.
4. Lower yourself slowly back to the starting position.
5. Repeat 5 to 10 times.

Calisthenic Exercise

Step 3

The Push-Up
(to strengthen arm, shoulder, chest and back muscles).
1. Lie flat on your stomach: legs together, toes touching the ground.
2. Place your hands flat on the floor, almost directly beneath your shoulders.
3. Push body up, keeping it straight at all times, until arms are fully straightened.
4. Slowly lower body, still keeping it perfectly straight, until you almost touch the floor.
5. Push body up again, and return again.
6. Repeat 5 times (without touching the floor between push-ups).

Calisthenic Exercise

Step 2

Alternate Arm Swing and Bounce
(to firm the leg muscles and improve shoulder flexibility).
1. Stand with the feet parallel, shoulder-width apart, and knees bent at a 45-degree angle. The body should lean forward and the arms and hands relaxed.
2. Swing one arm forward as the opposite swings back.
3. Continue by reversing the position of the arms with an easy swinging motion.
4. As the motion is continued, bend the knees more than the 45-degree angle and then straighten them. Try to coordinate arm and leg movements.
5. Repeat 10 times.

Calisthenic Exercise

Step 1

Punching Bag
(to help tone both the triceps and biceps muscles).
   1. Begin with the arms extended, and alternately
   drawing them back in front of the body. (Simulate
   punching a punching bag.) A drawing in toward the
   body and returning to an extended position
   constitutes one repetition.
   2. Repeat 10 times.

Calisthenic Exercise

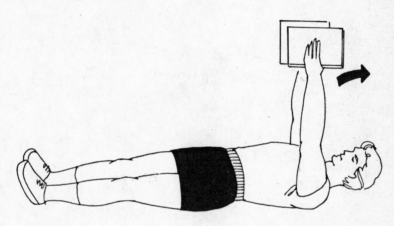

Step 2

Arms Over
(to strengthen the chest and arm muscles).
1. Hold a book in each hand (hands at sides) while lying on your back.
2. Raise the books over your head, reaching as far back as possible.
3. Then return hands to sides.
4. Perform 3 sets of 8 repetitions.

Calisthenic Exercise

Step 1

Right Angles
(to strengthen chest and arm muscles).
1. Lie on your back with your arms at right angles to your body and a book in each hand.
2. Raise your arms so that they come together (arms straight) above your chest.
3. Pull in your abdomen at the same time.
4. Return to starting position.
5. Perform 3 sets of 8 repetitions.

Calisthenic Exercise

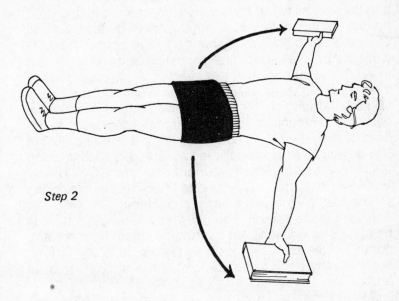

Step 2

Arm Arc
(to strengthen your chest and arm muscles).
1. Lie on your back with your arms extended toward your knees and a book in each hand.
2. Sweep your arms out to the sides as though you were making an arc to at least shoulder-height.
3. Return to starting position.
4. Perform 3 sets of 8 repetitions.

Where To Do It

THOUSANDS of people these days go to the YMCA, YWCA, local gym, or health club to work with weights. If you decide to go to such a club, it would be wise for you to evaluate their facilities and programs. If they cater only to the power lifters, it can be very self-defeating to struggle with 30 pounds while an experienced lifter is handling 200 pounds right next to you. But if they provide facilities and programs for both the beginner and the power lifter, the club atmosphere and group participation is good for motivational purposes.

There are several real advantages to establishing a "better body building center" in your own home. For instance, having equipment in your home means that you do not have to adjust your schedule to that of a large institution. Nor do you have to spend time traveling. Most importantly, at home you can execute your personalized CONSUMER GUIDE® program precisely, without feeling self-conscious or intimidated by more experienced lifters.

Where in the house, though? That's the question most beginners ask. Check out your home, room by room and corner by corner. We suggest a room about 20-by-15 feet, but you may have to be content with a smaller area, at least at the start.

If your house or apartment has large rooms, space will probably not be a problem. If you live in a small house or apartment, however, you will have to assess the possibility of converting an extra bedroom or part of the living room into your weight-training area. In an apartment the landlord might let you use part of the basement. A heated garage can also be converted into an exercise room, but keep in mind that it is important to have a place that allows you to work out no matter how cold or wet it is outside. It's also best if you avoid lifting on the second floor, for obvious reasons.

When choosing your weight-lifting site, always be sure the ceiling is high enough to permit you to extend your arms fully overhead. In addition, always lift weights over a mat; mats soften the impact of weights being set down or accidentally dropped and they also provide better traction for your shoes than a slick floor.

Ventilation and room temperature are also very important. Make sure your exercise space is well-ventilated, and try to keep the temperature between 68 and 70 degrees Fahrenheit. The air should be warm but not so warm as to be uncomfortable. Blasts of cold air, from an air conditioner during summer or an open window during winter, are to be avoided because of chilling.

What You Will Need

ONCE YOU have a room in which to exercise, you need to buy equipment. The first thing to purchase, of course, is a basic set of inexpensive barbells or dumbbells.

You will also need a mat and probably a bench, although you can get by without the bench at first. Shop around at sporting goods stores, department stores, and reputable catalog retailers (such as Sears and Montgomery Ward). Before you put your money down on any type of body-building gear, though, be sure to read the evaluations of CONSUMER GUIDE®'s experts in the section, "The CONSUMER GUIDE® Name-Brand Product Evaluation."

Weight training is based on
eight proven principles that
define how muscles respond
to the stress imposed on
them. Understanding those
eight principles is important
to anyone intending to build a
better body.

Principles
Of Training

WEIGHT TRAINING is a term that applies to the procedure of systematically conditioning the various muscles of your body. Such conditioning will improve muscular strength, endurance, size, and appearance.

The process of weight training is a deliberate one, requiring that you follow and understand eight important principles to achieve the most effective results. By reviewing these principles you will understand why you should follow certain procedures and why your body responds the way it does.

Adaptation

WHEN MUSCLES are subjected to the repeated lifting of a weight, they eventually adapt to that stress. If the body is made to work harder, it will soon be able to work harder. Generally, adaptation is measured by improvement in performance, a principle which is important in establishing an exercise program. Athletes know this vividly. Out of shape at the start of the season, they train for weeks to condition and harden their bodies. Their muscles adapt; they get into shape.

For example, suppose you are currently engaged in a weight-training program that involves curling 50 pounds 10 times. First the schedule may be quite demanding, leaving you virtually exhausted. But after a period of weeks you will find that the lift becomes easier and less fatiguing. In fact, 50 pounds 10 times soon becomes a piece of cake, your body having adapted to the stress imposed upon it.

Overload

THE OVERLOAD principle is basic to a weight-training program. Overloading means that when muscles are repeatedly and regularly stimulated by a greater-than-normal weight and number of exercises, they adjust and increase their capacity to perform physical work. If you want to improve your strength, therefore, your body must be repeatedly subjected to a weight-training routine more vigorous than normal. As soon as your body adapts to an exercise level, you must increase the work so that your body is stimulated by the greater-than-normal exercise load.

There are four ways to overload. The first is to increase the weight. The second is to increase the duration of the exercise. The third, which is implied in the second, involves increasing the number of repetitions. And the fourth is to increase both the weight and the length of time.

Proper overloading should be introduced gradually to permit adaptation to take place without undue strain on the body. Although it is normal to have some muscle soreness and tiredness at the start of training, overloading does not require you to suffer excessive discomfort to the point where you limit your daily activity.

Progression

THE GRADUAL approach to overloading and adapting is called progression, another weight training principle.

When you begin lifting, you find you are able to curl 50 pounds 10 times each day. Soon that level is no longer stressful to your body. Since your body has adapted, you progressively increase the weight by lifting 55 pounds 10 times. You have now overloaded the muscles once more. An alternative approach would be to lift 50 pounds 15 times.

Notice that in each instance the increases were rather small. They were what weight-training experts call progressive, meaning that the increments were significant enough to present a new challenge to the body but not enough to leave the person completely exhausted.

Progression enables you to increase your work load gradually. Muscles will not become sore, and the likelihood of overtaxing or even injuring the body during the training will be reduced. Failure to increase in a progressive manner can lead to frustration and pain.

Specificity

SPECIFICITY REFERS to the fact that improvements made in training are directly related to the type of training followed. For example, a strength training program (weight training) does not result in an increase in endurance. Similarly, a flexibility program like yoga does little to improve strength and endurance. By the same token, working one area of the body will not improve another area. If you spend all your time developing the upper body, for example, the muscles of your lower body will not benefit in the least.

Many athletes have experienced this phenomenon of specificity. Swimmers serve as a good example. The swimmer who considers himself to be in great condition finds that when he attempts to play a rigorous game of basketball he is forced to quit. The reason for the apparent lack of conditioning for basketball is due to the physiological principle of specificity.

Weight training is no different. You must work most of the major muscle groups of the body if you expect to develop total muscle fitness. You can't just work on the legs and expect your upper body to improve and vice versa.

Most importantly, you must understand that weight training does not condition or strengthen the heart and lungs, the keys to true physical fitness.

Retrogression

WHEN WEIGHT TRAINING, you may find that on certain days your performance seems to be off the usual pace. Try as you might you cannot curl 50 pounds 10 times, even though you have done this for the past three weeks. The reason for this decline or fall off in performance — called retrogression — is not known, but it probably has something to do with the ability of your body to mobilize its resources for meeting the overload imposed upon it. When the body adjusts, you then begin to reach your typical level of performance.

Occasionally, retrogression is the result of a poor diet, inadequate sleep or rest, lack of motivation, and/or improper conditioning or training. But regardless of the cause, it is important that you constantly monitor your current condition. Be sure that your nutritional intake is adequate, that your rest and sleep are sufficient, and that your training techniques are proper. If the retrogression is significant (more than a 10 percent decrease in performance in a week), reduce the degree of overload for a few days or switch to another activity. After the appraisal and tapering off, improvement is bound to follow. Don't be discouraged. Retrogression is a common experience to weight trainers.

Use And Disuse

THE SIXTH principle of training is that of use and disuse. If you require part of your body to perform a certain task, the efficiency of that part will remain the same or improve (use). Conversely, if you do not require a part of your body to perform a certain task, or other similar tasks, the efficiency of the part will degenerate (disuse). Muscles grow larger and stronger when exercised, while muscles that are underexercised decrease. In short, use promotes function, while disuse may reduce the ability to function.

Skill

MUCH OF THE improvement that occurs during the early stage of weight training must be attributed to improved skill in lifting. The improvement is the result of learning how to do the exercise or activity more efficiently. For example, the first time you try to bench press you may be able to lift no more than 50 pounds, but at the end of the week you are able to do 75 pounds. The improvement is due not so much to increased strength as to improved technique. Weight trainers recognize this phenomenon, and competitive lifters will spend a good deal of time improving their technique.

Individual Rates Of Response

INDIVIDUAL RATES of response is the eighth physiological principle of weight training. Each person has his or her own rate of response to the training program. Occasionally, some people seem to arrive at a high level of conditioning long before others. The reason for this difference is not clear. It is probably due to several variables, a few of which may be 1) present physical condition; 2) age; 3) body type; 4) weight; 5) rest, sleep, and relaxation; 6) nutrition; 7) freedom from disease; 8) proneness to injury; 9) motivation; and 10) the ability to learn new skills.

Weight-Training Approaches

THERE ARE three distinct approaches to weight training: strength, power, and endurance. The eight basic principles of training apply to each approach, although some may be emphasized more than others.

Strength is the ability (or inability) to lift an object with a muscle or group of muscles. To increase the strength of a muscle or muscle group requires that the muscle(s) be progressively overloaded. That is, they must be exercised against an increasing amount of resistance. Each time the body adapts to a certain resistance, additional resistance must be placed on the muscle so that it is consistently overloaded. The resistance may be isotonic (movement) or

Weight training, a form of isotonic exercise, is concerned with building muscle strength or endurance.

isometric (no movement).

Weight training is a form of isotonic exercise concerned with building muscle strength or endurance. There are several methods of weight training. Essentially, the idea is to find a desirable weight for each exercise, so that eight repetitions (and only eight repetitions) of a weight can be lifted. You work at that level on an alternate-day basis until you are able to perform three sets of eight repetitions. It may take days, weeks, or months to reach that goal. But when you achieve the goal, you add more weight so that you can execute a maximum of only eight repetitions. And then you repeat the entire cycle. As the muscle is overloaded, it adapts; more weight is added progressively, and the muscle is overloaded again. Research indicates that few repetitions (6 to 10) and high resistance executed on alternate days produce the best strength improvement.

A second major type of strength training involves isometric exercise. Here a muscle is exercised against an immovable object — a wall, a bar, or another muscle. Since the resistance is so great, no movement occurs, but the muscle grows in strength because it is overloaded.

Once a sufficient amount of muscular strength has been developed to perform a particular movement, it may be advantageous to work on increasing the speed of movement. The concentration on increasing movement speed is called power training, and it emphasizes explosiveness.

Generally, power training requires that you follow the

same program as for strength training except that you try to move the weight as rapidly as possible through its full range of motion. The emphasis is on high resistance, few repetitions, at a high speed. Alternate-day activities seem to be best.

Endurance training improves the capacity to perform work of moderate intensity for an extended period of time. There are two types of endurance — muscular and cardiovascular endurance. With weight training, the emphasis is on muscular endurance or the ability to perform repeated muscular exertions.

To build muscle endurance (and improve appearance and tone), you should lift a lighter weight many times. For example, you might try curling a weight of 30 pounds 15 repetitions for a maximum of three times. Speed is not a factor. You work at that level on an alternate-day basis until you are able to do three sets of 15 repetitions maximum. When you reach that level you then increase the weight and start the process all over again.

Weight training poses little
hazard to cautious
men and women who
learn proper lifting
techniques. Here are the
CONSUMER GUIDE®
body-building exercises and a
complete explanation of the
right way to do each one.

The Exercises And How To Do Them

WEIGHT training is one of the safest of all sports — provided that you observe the proper safety precautions. A survey of more than 30,000 weight lifters in YMCAs, clubs, and colleges showed a very low incidence of injuries directly related to this activity. Many of these injuries, moreover, consisted of nothing more than pulled muscles or tendons. Beginners, however, suffered numerous problems, an indication they were not lifting properly.

Proper technique is the key to safe and successful weight training. All strenuous physical activity has inherent in it some possible harm. Recognition of some possible dangers in weight training will enable you to get the maximum benefit out of the CONSUMER GUIDE® program without harming yourself. The first thing to do is make a thorough check of your equipment to be sure it is safe. The weights — even light ones — should be securely locked so that they can neither slide to one end nor fall.

The next thing to do is listen to your body. If you are not ready for weight training, or if you are proceeding too fast, your body will "talk" to you. It will send out signals that you should heed. Here are some of the basic signals.

Throbbing head

Chest pain

Arm pain

Persistent joint or muscle pain

Dizziness

Nausea

Abnormal strain

Abnormal breathlessness

These signals mean stop what you are doing and discuss what your body is saying with a doctor or some reputable exercise specialist or fitness authority. These signals may turn out to be nothing to worry about, but they may turn out to be signs of a physical problem. In either case, your doctor will be able to tell you what course of action to take.

Some Basic "Don'ts"

THE ONE crucial "do," of course, involves listening to your body. But there are also some basic "don'ts" involved in performing any of the lifts or exercises described in this chapter. Here are a few of them.

Don't hold your breath. Most people don't know how to breathe during strenuous exercise. Some believe that they should hold their breath while performing a lift, but holding your breath can impair your ability to follow through on the various lifts. Always continue to breathe regularly and deeply.

Don't use other muscle groups to help with a particular exercise or lift. From the techniques described and illustrated in this chapter you will learn which muscle group is affected by a given exercise. Cheating (i.e., leaning on other muscles or muscle groups) not only defeats the purpose of your exercise but also can harm the muscles you misuse.

Don't fail to go through the full range of motion. You will be cheating yourself if you do not exercise the muscle or muscle group through the full range of motion. You will lose flexibility. For the least risk of injury, the technique shown should be followed.

Don't overdo. Beginners often get impatient. They push themselves to move at a faster pace than the program recommends. Avoid the temptation to overdo. Proceed at a steady, comfortable pace — at your level — and you will make progress both quickly and safely.

Don't work alone. The experienced weight lifter is able to work safely alone, but the beginner should have a partner to help out in case difficulties arise. This is especially true if you are using relatively heavy weights or performing potentially dangerous lifts. It shouldn't be hard to find a friend who wants to participate in a program of building a better body.*

Don't lift with your back. Some people tend to "put their back into it" when performing lifts or exercises intended for other muscle groups. Such misuse of the back muscles can lead to problems with the lower back. Lift with your legs.

In essence, then, the best way to get the most out of body building is to follow the exercises presented here precisely as they are described. Don't cheat, take any short cuts, or improvise. Instead, trust in those who have experimented, tested, and developed the techniques we describe and illustrate.

* As a general rule, you should have a partner with you when lifting any weight in excess of 30 pounds (if you're a woman) or 40 pounds (if you're a man) over your head or above your chest.

Exercise For The Neck

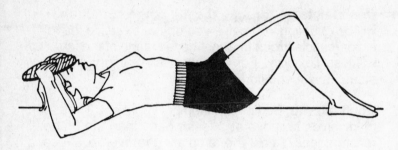

Step 2

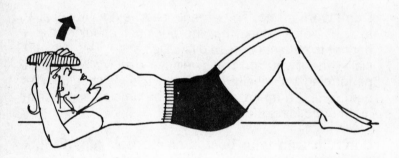

Step 3

Neck Curl
(to develop muscles that draw head forward).
1. Lie on back with legs either straight or bent.
2. Hold weight (plate) in place on forehead with both hands.
3. Curl head forward until chin touches throat or as far as possible.
4. Return slowly to the starting position.

Exercise For The Neck

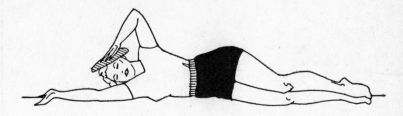

Step 2

Step 3

Side Neck Lift
(to develop muscles that draw head to the side).
    1. Lie on side.
    2. Hold weight (plate) on the side of the head.
    3. Lift head upward and sideward as far as possible.
    4. Return slowly to the original position.
    5. Repeat on the other side.

Exercise For The Neck

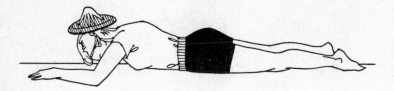

Step 2

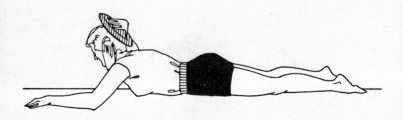

Step 3

Neck Extension
(to develop muscles that draw head backward).
1. Lie on stomach: face to the ground, legs and toes touching floor.
2. Grasp weight (plate) and place on back of head.
3. Lift head backward and upward as high as possible.
4. Return slowly to the starting position.

Exercise For The Shoulders, Back, Chest And Arms

Step 2   Step 3

Arm Press
(to develop muscles of shoulders, upper back, upper chest, and back of upper arms).
1. Stand with feet apart.
2. Hold barbell in front of chest, using overhand grip.
3. Extend the barbell over the head, keeping arms straight.
4. Return the barbell to the starting position.

Exercise For The Chest, Shoulders, And Arms

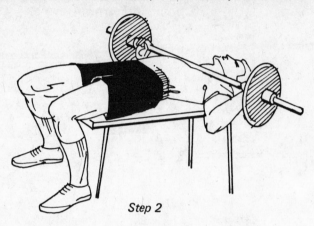

Step 2

Step 3

Bench Press

(to develop muscles of chest, front shoulders, and back of upper arms).

1. Assume a supine position on a bench: knees bent, feet flat on the floor.
2. Hold barbell across chest, overhand grip.
3. Press barbell upward until arms are fully extended.
4. Return barbell slowly to starting position.

Exercise For The Shoulders

Step 2   Step 3

Lateral Raise
(to develop muscles either on top of the shoulders or which cap the shoulders).
1. Stand with feet slightly apart.
2. Hold dumbbells down at the sides of your body in overhand grip.
3. Lift dumbbells sideways to a horizontal level — or beyond, if you comfortably can, to an overhead position.
4. Return to starting position.

Exercise For The Shoulders And Neck

Step 2

Shoulder Shrug
(to develop muscles of upper shoulders and side of the neck).
    1. Stand with feet apart: arms extended downward.

Exercise For The Shoulders And Neck

Step 3

2. Hold barbell in overhand grip, resting against thighs.
3. Lift the shoulders; try to touch the top of the shoulders
   to the ears.
4. Return slowly to the original position.

Exercise For The Shoulders, Back And Arms

Step 1

Rowing

(to develop muscles of back, back of shoulders, and front of upper arms).

(Anyone who has a history of back pain should avoid this exercise.)

   1. Stand with your feet apart: trunk bent at a 90-degree angle, knees and back straight.

Exercise For The Shoulders, Back And Arms

Step 3

2. Grasp the barbell at a little more than shoulder width in overhand grip, arms straight.
3. Lift barbell by bending the elbows and bringing the bar all the way to the chest.
4. Return to starting position.

Exercise For The Shoulders And Back

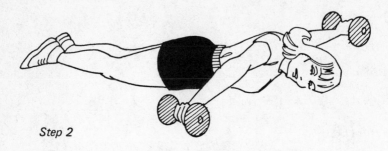

Step 2

Step 3

Prone Arm Lift
(to develop muscles of upper back and back of shoulders).
   1. Assume a prone position on the floor: arms extended
      at right angles to the body.
   2. Grasp the dumbbells with overhand grip.
   3. Raise arms as high as possible, toward the ceiling.
   4. Lower them slowly back to the original position.

Exercise For The Chest And Arms

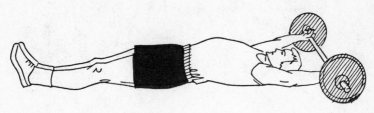

Step 2

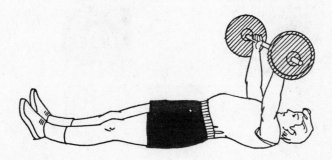

Step 3

Supine Pull-Over
(to develop muscles of the front of chest, back of upper arms, and sides of chest).
1. Assume a supine position on a bench or floor: arms extended out beyond the head parallel to the body.
2. Hold barbell with overhand grip.
3. Raise arms to a 90-degree angle directly overhead: keep arms straight.
4. Return barbell to original position, keeping arms straight.

Exercise For The Chest And Shoulders

Step 2

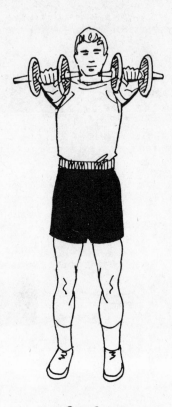

Step 3

Forward Raise
(to develop muscles of upper chest and front of shoulders).
1. Stand with feet apart.
2. Hold dumbbells down at the sides of body in overhand grip.
3. Raise dumbbells forward to shoulder height keeping the arms straight.
4. Lower dumbbells to original position.

Exercise For The Arms

Step 1

Step 2

Barbell Curls
(to develop muscles of the front of upper arms, forearms).
1. Stand with feet shoulder width apart, arms at sides. Hold barbell against the thighs in underhand grip.
2. Flex forearms, raising barbell to shoulders.
3. Return to starting position.

Exercise For The Arms

Step 2

Step 3

Reverse Curl
(to develop muscles of upper arms and back of forearms).
1. Stand with feet apart.
2. Hold barbell directly in front of your thighs in overhand grip.
3. Bring bar up to shoulders (as in arm curl, except that this time you are using the overhand grip).
4. Return to starting position.

Exercise For The Arms

Step 2

Step 3

Triceps Press
(to develop muscles of upper arms).
1. Stand with feet apart.
2. Hold dumbbells overhead.
3. Lower dumbbells slowly behind neck, bending elbows
   (as the weight is brought down toward the shoulder,
   the elbows will tend to point toward the ceiling).
4. Return to starting position.

Exercise For The Arms And Hands

Step 3

Wrist Curl
(to develop flexor muscles of forearms and hands).
   1. Sit on bench: forearms resting on thighs, wrists
      extended beyond knees.

Exercise For The Arms And Hands

Step 4

2. Hold barbell in underhand grip.
3. Extend hands at the wrists, lowering bar as far as possible toward the floor.
4. Flex wrists, bringing bar upward as far as possible.
5. Return to starting position.

Exercise For The Arms And Hands

Step 2

Wrist Extensor
(to develop extensor muscles of forearms and hands).
1. Sit on bench: forearms resting on your thighs, wrists extended beyond the knees.
2. Hold the barbell in overhand grip.

Exercise For The Forearms

Step 3

3. Lift the bar by extending the wrists upward through their maximum range of movement: do not lift your forearms.
4. Return to starting position.

Exercise For The Forearms

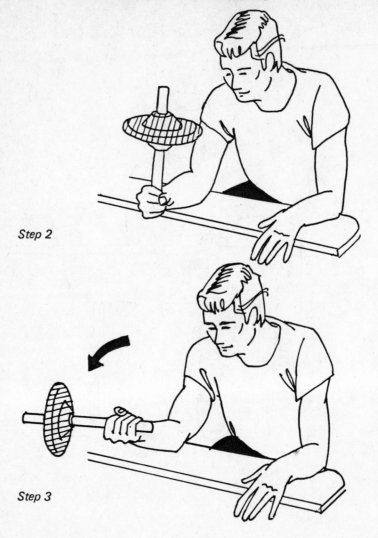

Step 2

Step 3

Supinator-Pronator
(to develop supinator and pronator muscles of forearms).
1. Sit on bench: forearm on table, only wrist and hand extended beyond the support.
2. With an overhand grip, grasp a dumbbell weighted on only one end in an upright position.

Exercise For The Forearms

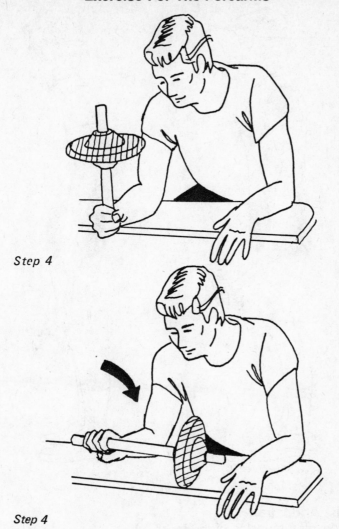

Step 4

Step 4

3. Lower weight to one side so that palm is facing upward.
4. Return dumbbell to an upright position, then lower it to other side so that palm is facing downward.
5. Repeat, using the other arm.

Exercise For The Forearms

Step 2

Step 3

Wrist Abduction
(to develop muscles of the forearm).
1. Stand with feet apart.
2. Load dumbbell at one end only, grasp it at other end in overhand grip.
3. Allow dumbbell to drop slowly in an arc until it points to the floor.
4. Return dumbbell to its original position.
5. Repeat, using other arm.

Exercise For The Arms

Step 2   *Step 3*

Wrist Adduction
(to develop wrist muscles).
1. Stand with feet apart.
2. Grasp dumbbell loaded at one end as in Wrist Abduction exercise: point loaded end to the rear.
3. Allow dumbbell to drop slowly in an arc until it points to the floor.
4. Return it in the same arc to the original position.
5. Repeat, using other arm.

Exercise For The Arms And Hands

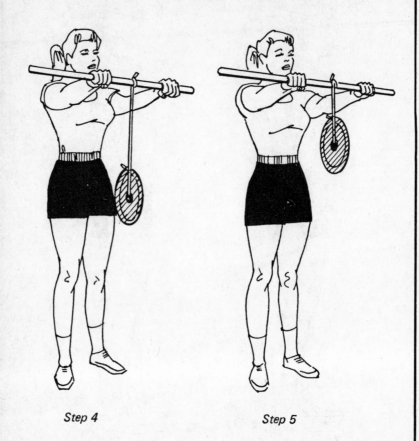

Step 4   Step 5

Wrist Roller
(to develop muscles of hands, wrists and forearms).
1. Fasten rope or strong cord to the center of cylindrical handle about 12 inches long (dumbbell bar works fine).
2. Tie weight (plate) to the opposite end of the rope.
3. Stand with feet shoulder-width apart.
4. Grasp ends of bar with overhand grip.
5. Roll the rope onto the handle.
6. Slowly reverse the movement, allowing the weight to return to the starting position.

Exercise For The Abdomen

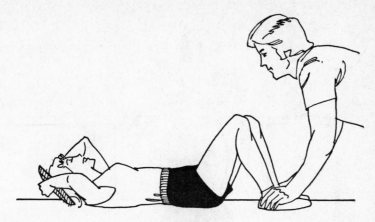

Step 1

Step 3

Sit-Ups
(to develop abdominal muscles)
1. Lie on back: knees bent, feet held in place by barbell or by assistant.
2. Grasp a weight (plate) behind head.
3. Sit up, touching the left elbow to the right knee, and then the right elbow to the left knee.
4. Return to original position.

Exercise For The Abdomen

Step 2

Side Bend
(to develop muscles on sides of abdomen).
    1. Stand with feet a little wider than shoulder-width apart.

Exercise For The Shoulders

Step 3

2. Hold in overhand grip, barbell resting on shoulders.
3. Bend body to the left side as far as possible.
4. Return carefully to the erect position.
5. Repeat the exercise on the other side.

Exercise For The Abdomen

Step 2

Step 4

Leg Press Out
(to develop muscles of abdomen and upper legs).
1. Wear weighted shoes or heavy boots.
2. Sit on floor with hands directly behind the buttocks.
3. Tuck legs up and allow all body weight to rest on the buttocks and the hands.
4. Press legs together and slowly straighten outward until fully extended and approximately 8 to 12 inches above the floor.

Exercise For The Hips And Pelvis

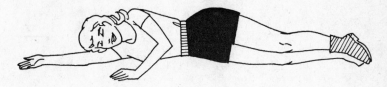

Step 2

Step 3

Hip Abductor
(to develop muscles on side of hips).
1. Wear weighted shoe or heavy boot.
2. Lie on side: the under arm extended above head, the top arm across the front of body for support.
3. Raise top leg as far as possible, working toward an angle of 45 degrees or more.
4. Lower leg slowly to original position. (Keep the knee extended at all times during the movement).
5. Repeat exercise on other side with other leg.

Dual-Resistance
Exercise For The Hips And Legs

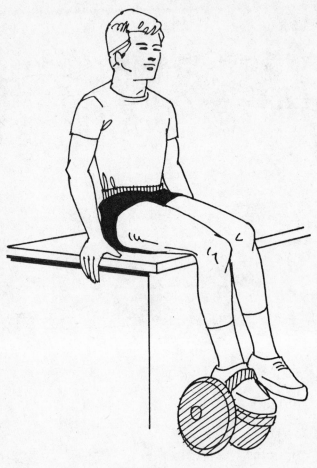

Step 2

Hip Flexor
(to develop muscles of front of hips and upper legs).
   1. Wear weighted shoe or heavy boot.
   2. Sit on table: edge of table should touch back of knees.

Dual-Resistance
Exercise For The Hips And Legs

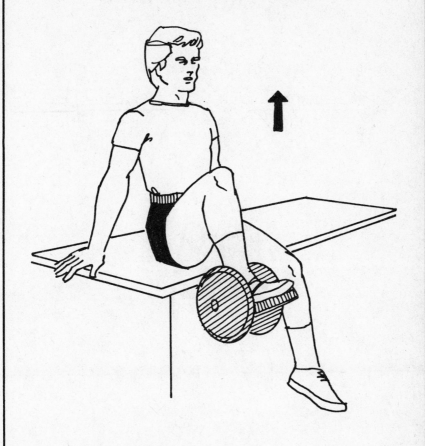

Step 4

3. Grasp edges of the table with hands.
4. Raise knee towards the chest, as far as possible. (Do not bend body forward or backward).
5. Lower knee slowly.
6. Repeat with other knee.

Step 1

One-Half Squat
(to develop muscles of front thigh and lower leg).
  1. Stand with feet comfortably spread. Hold barbell in
      overhand grip behind the neck, resting on shoulders.

Exercise For The Legs

Step 2

2. Bend knees to perform a half-squat (90 degrees).
3. Return to the starting position.

Exercise For The Legs And Back

Step 3

Straddle Lift
(to develop muscles of upper and lower legs and lower back).

(Anyone who has had a hernia should avoid this exercise.)
    1. Stand with one foot slightly in front of the other.
    2. Crouch, legs straddling barbell.

Exercise For The Legs And Back

Step 4

3. Grasp the bar with alternate grip, one hand in front of body, one behind.
4. Extend knees and trunk, coming to an erect position. (Keep head up and back straight).
5. Return to crouch position.

Exercise For The Legs

Step 2

Step 3

Walking Squat
(to develop muscles of upper and lower legs).
1. Stand with one foot 12 to 18 inches in front of the other.
2. Hold barbell in overhand grip behind neck, resting on shoulders.
3. Take one step forward, executing a half-knee-bend (thighs parallel to the floor).
4. Return to upright position.
5. Repeat exercise with other leg.

Exercise For The Legs

Step 2

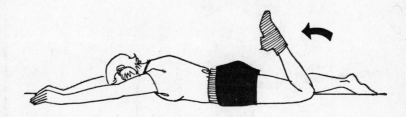

Step 3

Knee Curl
(to develop muscles of back of leg).
1. Wear weighted shoe or heavy boot.
2. Assume a prone position on a bench or the floor: hands extended above head.
3. Curl one leg upward until the boot nearly or actually touches the buttocks.
4. Slowly return to original position.
5. Repeat exercise with other leg.

Exercise For The Legs

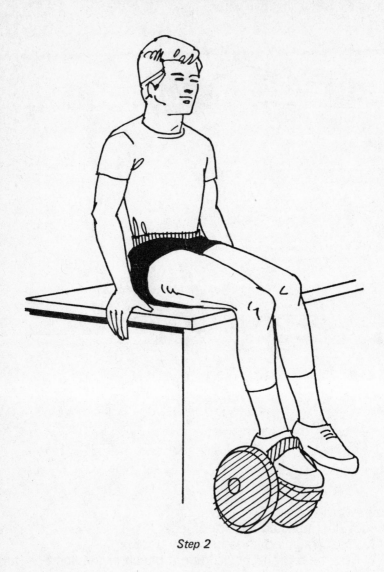

Step 2

Sitting Leg Raise
(to develop the muscles on the front of the thigh).
1. Wear weighted shoe or heavy boot.
2. Sit on edge of table: legs hanging over edge.

Exercise For The Legs

Step 3

3. Raise one leg to a horizontal position by straightening the knee.
4. Return slowly to starting position.
5. Repeat exercise with other leg.

Exercise For The Legs

Step 1

Step 3

Toe Raise
(to develop muscles of the back of lower leg).
1. Stand with balls of feet on a 1- to 2-inch block of wood (or a book); heels on floor.
2. Hold barbell in overhand grip behind neck, resting on shoulders.
3. Raise up on toes as far as possible.
4. Return to original position.

Exercise For The Legs And Ankles

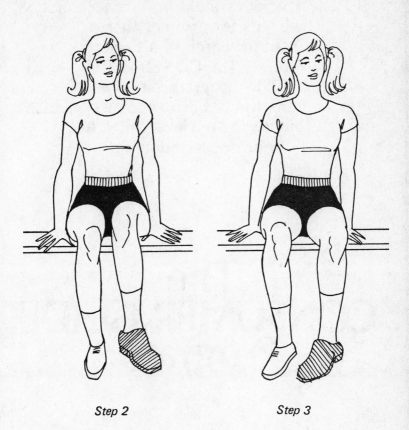

Step 2   *Step 3*

Ankle Turn
(to develop muscles of ankle joints and the front of lower legs).
1. Wear weighted shoe or heavy boot.
2. Sit on table: legs hanging over end of table.
3. Turn one foot inward and then outward as far as possible.
4. Return to original position.
5. Repeat exercise with other foot.

A woman seeking greater
strength should lift heavier
weights fewer times than a
man in search of a firmer
torso. The CONSUMER
GUIDE® program shows you
how to establish your own
routine, the one best suited to
your needs and goals.

The
CONSUMER GUIDE®
Program

BUILDING A BETTER BODY is the name of the CON-
SUMER GUIDE® program because that is precisely
what this group of weight-training exercises is designed to
do. Regardless of your sex or age, you can build a better
body by following the guidelines and approaches
presented in this chapter. But it is you who must tailor the

execution of the program to meet your own personal needs.

You must ask yourself: What do you want from the program; where should you begin; and at what rate should you progress?

The three approaches offered here are based on different goals. Each approach involves exercising with weights, but each is different in the results it is designed to produce. The first, for example, is designed to tone your body; the second to build muscular strength; while the third is designed to build power — a combination of muscular strength and speed. You select what you want to achieve for your own body, and proceed from there. If you want all three results, you begin working with the first approach then move in order to the second and third.

In this chapter, you will learn step-by-step procedures for determining where you should begin, how you should tailor or individualize each aspect of the program, and what methods you should use to apply the approach (or approaches) you decide to pursue. The specific techniques for each exercise are described and illustrated in detail in the chapter entitled "The Exercises And How To Do Them."

A Checklist of Weight-Training Hazards. . .

– Don't overdo ("Train, don't strain.")
– Follow the prescribed exercise techniques exactly.
– Be sure to go through the full range of motion.
– Do not cheat by using other muscle groups to help you with a particular lift.
– Do not hold your breath while lifting.
– Do not use poor or damaged equipment.
– Be certain that equipment is properly assembled.
– Do not lift with your back.
– Have a partner with you if you are lifting relatively heavy weights.

Some Preliminaries

IN ORDER to achieve the best results from any exercise program, it is necessary to set up and follow a specific schedule. The CONSUMER GUIDE® program prescribes just such a schedule: exercise three days a week — and only three days — with at least one full day of rest between any two exercise sessions. You can work out on a Monday/Wednesday/Friday schedule or Saturday/Tuesday/Thursday combination, but do not skip the day of rest. The safest and most effective way to build your body through weight training requires that you allow your muscles to rest at least one full day between exercise sessions.

Setting up a firm weekly schedule is mandatory, but setting aside the specific time of day that you exercise on each of the three days can remain flexible. Usually, however, selecting a specific time of day for exercising and adhering to that time is the best way to guarantee that you will persist with your program. Once you get into the habit of exercising at a particular time, other interests and chores can be scheduled around your exercise time, rather than vice versa.

There are two times, however, that are not good for exercising. Avoid workouts immediately before going to bed and within an hour after eating a full meal.

The CONSUMER GUIDE® Program

HERE IS how the program works.

1. Select either Approach 1 (Exercising For Body Toning And Appearance), Approach 2 (Exercising For Strength), or Approach 3 (Exercising For Power).

2. Select a minimum of six exercises, but no more than 10, from the list provided in this chapter.

3. Read and understand the technique for each exercise you have selected, as illustrated and defined in the chapter "The Exercises And How To Do Them."

4. Test yourself to find the starting point for your individual exercise program.

5. Begin your own personal weight-training program.

Approach 1: Exercising For Body Toning And Appearance

IF YOUR body is not all you want it to be in terms of shape, firmness, and attractiveness, then Approach 1 is the one for you. It is designed to firm up sags, to tone the physique, and to add muscle in areas where it should be. In this part of the program you will lift relatively lighter weights, but you will repeat each lift more times than you would if you were following Approach 2 or Approach 3.

Approach 2: Exercising For Strength

IF YOUR body is deficient in overall strength and you want to overcome this weakness, then Approach 2 is the one for you. This part of the program focuses on building each muscle or muscle group so that it becomes stronger and therefore able to handle difficult tasks more easily. You will lift relatively heavier weights, but you will lift them fewer times than you would if you were following Approach 1.

Approach 3: Exercising For Power

APPEARANCE and strength are relatively self-explanatory concepts. Power, though, is not quite so easily understood. Power includes strength, but it refers to more than the ability of an Olympic weight lifter to hoist incredible poundage. Power, in this context, combines strength with speed — a combination appreciated by anyone who participates in sports. In this part of the program, you will lift relatively heavier weights, but at a much faster rate of speed than you would if you were following Approach 1 or Approach 2.

Selecting Your Lifts

NOW IT is time to tailor your own program. You know best which body areas and muscle groups need work. If they all do, select an exercise from each body area category. In this way, you can work on all body muscle groups. If there are just certain areas to be improved, simply concentrate on them.

The exercises themselves vary, although not to a large degree, in difficulty and rigor. In each group the easier exercises are listed first, with the more difficult ones following. You need not, however, start out with the easiest; in fact, we recommend that you choose those exercises you most want to do and find the most comfortable and satisfying. Since you will start at a proper level for your body condition, there is little chance you will overdo — no matter which exercises you select — so long as you adhere to the CONSUMER GUIDE® program.

Once into the program, you can make changes, substituting different exercises within a group. In fact, such alteration adds variety to your exercise activities without detracting from the results you want to achieve.

From the following list, select at least six — but not more than 10 — exercises with which you would like to start your program. It would be wise at this point to go back and check each exercise in the chapter "The Exercises And How To Do Them" to be certain you know everything that is involved.

Testing Yourself

ONCE YOU decide on your program and the specific lifting exercises, you must determine just where to begin. Where you begin is actually the basis for tailoring the program to your sex, age, and physical condition. Each person starts at his or her own level, the level at which he or she feels comfortable. Rate of progress is an individual matter, suited to individual capability. This is why the CONSUMER GUIDE® program is truly an individualized approach to building a better body.

For each lift you have selected there is a "Recommended Testing Weight" for men and women. This figure, which represents the combined weight of the bar and weight plates, is the weight you should use first to test your capabilities.

RECOMMENDED TESTING WEIGHTS (POUNDS)

Exercise	Men	Women
For the Neck:		
1. Neck Curl	5	2 ½
2. Side Neck Lift	5	2 ½
3. Neck Extension	5	2 ½
For the Shoulders:		
4. Arm Press	40 *	20 *
5. Bench Press	50 *	30 *
6. Lateral Raise	5	2 ½
7. Shoulder Shrug	40 *	20 *
8. Rowing	30	20
9. Prone Arm Lift	5	2 ½
For the Chest:		
10. Supine Pull-Over	10	5
11. Forward Raise	5	2 ½
For the Upper Arms:		
12. Barbell Curls	30	20
13. Reverse Curl	30	20
14. Triceps Press	7 ½	2 ½
For the Forearms:		
15. Wrist Curl	10	5
16. Wrist Extensor	10	5
17. Supinator-Pronator	5	2 ½
18. Wrist Abduction	5	2 ½
19. Wrist Adduction	5	2 ½
20. Wrist Roller	2 ½	1 **

You should have a partner when attempting these lift exercises.

** *One-pound weights are often not available. Use a one-pound book instead.*

RECOMMENDED TESTING WEIGHT (POUNDS)

Exercise	Men	Women
For the Abdomen:		
21. Sit-Ups	0 +	0 +
22. Side Bend	40 *	30 *
23. Leg Press Out	5	2 ½
For the Hips and Pelvis:		
24. Hip Abductor	10	5
25. Hip Flexor	10	5
For the Thighs and Lower Legs		
26. One-Half Squat	50 *	40 *
27. Straddle Lift	40 *	30 *
28. Walking Squat	50 *	30 *
29. Knee Curl	10	5
30. Sitting Leg Raise	10	5
31. Toe Raise	60 *	40 *
32. Ankle Turn	10	5

You should have a partner when attempting these lift exercises.

+ *Try first without weights (regular sit-up).*

Here's what you should do to test yourself and determine the weight level with which you should exercise.

With each exercise you select, find the number of pounds you can lift eight times or repetitions. Those eight repetitions represent the maximum you should attempt. You'll have to "guesstimate" the number of pounds in the beginning, but if you find that eight repetitions at that weight are too light, put on more weight. If you cannot do eight repetitions, the testing weight is too heavy. Rest several minutes, take off some weight, and try again.

It will take you several days to determine your best weight for each lift. But don't worry. That will be a good time to become familiar with the weights, to learn how to lift them, understand your body a little bit more, and start to prepare your muscles for more vigorous lifting. Don't view the first few days as time lost. It is time well spent.

Once you establish poundage for each of your 6 to 10 lifts, you are ready to begin. Record the poundage for each lift on the appropriate chart under the part of the program you have selected to follow. Once you've done that, you have adjusted the program for all your personal characteristics. You are ready, in other words, to begin your own body-building program.

The procedure for all three approaches to body building is quite simple. You select Approach 1 (Body Toning and Appearance), Approach 2 (Strength), or Approach 3 (Power), and then you do the specified number of repetitions for each lift three times. You do not proceed to a higher weight until you are able to perform three sets of the specified number of repetitions — 8 or 15. When you are able to do the required number, you add more weight and start the cycle once more for that lift.

Approach 1: Exercising For Body Toning And Appearance

Schedule: Three exercise sessions a week, with at least one day of rest between each session. All exercises selected (up to 15 repetitions) will be done at each session.

Starting Point: Take the test weight you determined and reduce it by 25 percent. If you tested out at 30 pounds, for example, your starting point will be 22½ pounds.

Program:
   1. Lifting the reduced test weight, you should be able to perform a maximum of 15 repetitions. You're not racing against time, but the repetitions must be done in a consecutive fashion. If you are able to do

Approach 1: Exercising For
Body Toning And Appearance

Exercise: _____

Testing Weight _____

Less 25% (or more) _____

	No. of pounds	Repetitions	Goal
Sequence 1	_____	15	15
Sequence 2	_____	_____	15
Sequence 3	_____	_____	15

Exercise: _____

Testing Weight _____

Less 25% (or more) _____

	No. of pounds	Repetitions	Goal
Sequence 1	_____	15	15
Sequence 2	_____	_____	15
Sequence 3	_____	_____	15

Exercise: _____

Testing _____

Less 25% (or more) _____

	No. of pounds	Repetitions	Goal
Sequence 1	_____	15	15
Sequence 2	_____	_____	15
Sequence 3	_____	_____	15

more than 15 repetitions, the weight is not heavy enough. If you cannot do 15 repetitions, the weight is too heavy.

2. Rest one minute after the 15 repetitions. A good

way to relax is simply to shake your arms and legs.
3. Repeat the 15 repetitions. No more. You'll probably be able to do somewhere between 10 to 12 repetitions.
4. Rest one minute.
5. Repeat the exercise. Now you will probably be able to do somewhere between 7 and 10 repetitions.
6. Rest two minutes.
7. Proceed to the next exercise in your program, following the same procedure for each. Allow two minutes of rest between each exercise set.

Progression: When you can do 15 repetitions of each of the three sequences for any given exercise, add five pounds to the barbell or dumbbell. Continue to increase the weight in this manner as long as you can lift the weights for the prescribed 15 repetitions in each set without excessive pain.

Approach 2: Exercising For Strength

Schedule: Three exercise sessions a week, with at least one full day of rest between each session. All exercises selected (up to 8 repetitions) will be done each session.

Starting Point: Use the exact weight that you determined during the testing phase.

Program:
1. Perform eight repetitions of each exercise at a rate you feel is comfortable. Speed is not the goal here. Your goal is eight repetitions, maximum. If you can do more, the weight is not heavy enough. If you can do fewer, you'll have to reduce the weight.
2. Rest one minute.
3. Attempt eight more repetitions of the exercise. You'll probably be able to do somewhere between five and six repetitions.
4. Rest one minute.
5. Perform as many repetitions (up to eight) of the exercise as you can. You'll probably be able to do somewhere between three and five repetitions.
6. Rest two minutes.

Approach 2: Exercising For Strength

Exercise: _____

Testing Weight _____

	No. of Pounds	Repetitions	Goal	Time Period
Sequence 1	_____	8	8	_____
Sequence 2	_____	_____	8	_____
Sequence 3	_____	_____	8	_____

Exercise: _____

Testing Weight _____

	No. of Pounds	Repetitions	Goal	Time Period
Sequence 1	_____	8	8	_____
Sequence 2	_____	_____	8	_____
Sequence 3	_____	_____	8	_____

Exercise: _____

Testing Weight _____

	No. of Pounds	Repetitions	Goal	Time Period
Sequence 1	_____	8	8	_____
Sequence 2	_____	_____	8	_____
Sequence 3	_____	_____	8	_____

7. Proceed to the next exercise in your program, following the same procedure for each, and allowing two minutes rest between each exercise set.

Progression: When you can do eight repetitions in each of the three sets for any given exercise, add five pounds to the barbell or dumbbell. Continue to increase the weight in this manner as long as you can perform the prescribed sequence of repetitions without excessive pain.

Approach 3: Exercising For Power

Exercise: _____

Testing Weight _____

	No. of Pounds	Repetitions	Goal	Time Period (seconds)	Time Limit (seconds)
Sequence 1	_____	8	8	_____	10
Sequence 2	_____	_____	8	_____	10
Sequence 3	_____	_____	8	_____	10

Exercise: _____

Testing Weight _____

	Pounds	Repetitions	Goal	Time Period (seconds)	Time Limit (seconds)
Sequence 1	_____	8	8	_____	10
Sequence 2	_____	8	8	_____	10
Sequence 3	_____	8	8	_____	10

Exercise: _____

Testing Weight _____

	Pounds	Repetitions	Goal	Time Period (seconds)	Time Limit (seconds)
Sequence 1	_____	8	8	_____	10
Sequence 2	_____	_____	8	_____	10
Sequence 3	_____	_____	8	_____	10

Approach 3: Exercising For Power

Schedule: Three exercise sessions a week, with at least one full day of rest between each session. All exercises selected (up to 8 repetitions) will be done at each session.

Starting Point: Use the exact weight that you determined during the testing phase.

Program:

1. Perform eight repetitions of each exercise within a time period not to exceed 10 seconds. You must go through the full range of motion for each repetition. If you can do more than eight repetitions in that period of time, the weight is not heavy enough. If you cannot perform the eight repetitions, though, you must reduce the weight.
2. Rest one minute.
3. Perform a maximum of eight repetitions of the exercise (or as many as you can without undue pain within the 10-second time limit). You'll probably be able to do around five or six.
4. Rest one minute.
5. Perform eight more repetitions of the exercise (or as many as you can without undue strain within the 10-second limit.) You will probably be able to perform between four and five repetitions.
6. Rest two minutes.
7. Proceed to the next exercise in your program, following the same procedure for each and allowing two minutes rest between each exercise set.

Progression: When you can do eight repetitions in 10 seconds or less in each of the three sets for any given exercise, add five pounds to the barbell or dumbbells. Continue to increase the weight in this manner as long as you can perform the sequence of repetitions within the prescribed time limit without excessive fatigue and pain.

Tailoring Your Weight Training For Sports And Other Activities

THE CONSUMER GUIDE® program can be utilized for development of those muscles you use when participating in particular sports or other activities. Tennis players, for example, may want to strengthen their arm muscles in order to deliver more powerful serves. Bicyclists may want stronger legs to improve their endurance in cycling. Householders may want to strengthen arms, legs, and shoulders to handle everyday chores with less strain and fatigue.

In order to help you improve specific muscles and muscle groups, we have listed below a wide variety of sports and activities. Under each is a list of the muscle areas that you should work on for improved performance. Simply select the appropriate weight-training exercises from the chapter "The Exercises And How To Do Them," then work on the appropriate areas. The best methods for improving these areas will be found in Approach 2 (Exercising For Strength) or Approach 3 (Exercising For Power).

SPORT

Archery
Neck, shoulders, biceps, triceps, forearms, wrists, abdomen, trunk

Backpacking
Neck, shoulders, upper arms, chest, abdomen, lower back, hip and pelvic muscles, thighs, lower legs and ankles

Badminton
Neck, shoulders, chest, upper arms, forearms, abdomen, lower back, thighs

Baseball (or Softball)
Shoulders, arms, chest, wrists, lower back, thighs, lower legs

Basketball
Shoulders, chest, forearms, wrists, abdomen, thighs, lower legs

Bicycling
Shoulders, abdomen, lower back, hips and pelvis, thighs, lower legs

Bowling
Shoulders, upper arms, forearms and wrists, abdomen, thighs

Boxing
Include all muscle groups

Canoeing (and Kayaking)
Shoulders, upper arms, forearms and wrists, abdomen, thighs

Cross-Country Skiing
(see Skiing, Snow and Water)

Diving
Neck, shoulders, chest, upper arms, forearms and wrists, abdomen, lower back, thighs, lower legs

Fencing
Shoulders, chest, upper arms, forearms, wrists, abdomen, lower back, thighs

Field Hockey
Shoulders, chest, upper arms, abdomen, thighs, lower legs, ankles

Football
Neck, shoulders, chest, forearms, wrists, abdomen, lower back, thighs, lower legs, ankles

Golf
Shoulders, chest, forearms, abdomen, lower back, thighs

Gymnastics
Neck, shoulders, chest, upper arms, forearms, abdomen, lower back, thighs

Handball
Shoulders, chest, upper arms, forearms and wrists, lower back, thighs

Ice Hockey
Shoulders, upper arms, forearms, abdomen, lower back, thighs, lower legs and ankles

Ice Skating
(see Skating)

Jai Alai
Shoulders, chest, upper arms, abdomen, lower back, thighs, lower legs

Kayaking
(see Canoeing)

Lacrosse
Neck, shoulders, upper arms, forearms, wrists, abdomen, lower back, thighs, lower legs, ankles

Racquetball
Shoulders, chest, upper arms, forearms and wrists, lower back, thighs

Roller Skating
(see Skating)

Rowing
Shoulders, upper arms, chest, abdomen, lower back, hips and pelvic muscles, thighs, lower legs

Running
Shoulders, abdomen, thighs, lower legs, ankles

Sailing
Shoulders, upper arms, forearms, abdomen, lower back, thighs

Scuba Diving
(see Skin Diving)

Shooting
Shoulders, chest, upper arms, abdomen, thighs

Skating
Upper arms, abdomen, lower back, hip and pelvic muscles, thighs, lower legs

Skiing, Snow and Water
Shoulders, upper arms, abdomen, lower back, hip and pelvic muscles, thighs, lower legs

Skin and Scuba Diving
Neck, shoulders, chest, upper arms, abdomen, lower back, thighs

Soccer
Neck, shoulders, chest, upper arms, abdomen, lower back, hips and pelvis, thighs, lower legs

Softball
(see Baseball)

Swimming
Neck, shoulders, chest, upper arms, forearms, abdomen, lower back, thighs

Tennis
Neck, shoulders, chest, upper arms, forearms, abdomen, lower back, thighs

Volleyball
Shoulders, upper arms, forearms, abdomen, hips, pelvis, thighs, lower legs

Water Skiing
(see Skiing, Snow and Water)

HOUSEHOLD CHORES

Carrying (a child, groceries, etc.)
Shoulders, upper arms, forearms, abdomen, lower back, hip and pelvic muscles, thighs, lower legs.

Ironing
Neck, shoulders, upper arms, forearms, wrists, abdomen, chest, lower back, thighs

Moving furniture
Shoulders, chest, upper arms, forearms, abdomen, lower back, hip and pelvic muscles, thighs

Painting walls and ceilings
Shoulders, neck, upper arms, forearms, wrists, hips and pelvis, thighs, lower legs, ankles

Washing walls or windows
Shoulders, upper arms, forearms, abdomen, hips and pelvis, thighs

Vacuuming
Shoulders, upper arms, forearms, chest, abdomen

OUTDOOR CHORES

Chopping wood
Shoulders, upper arms, forearms, abdomen, thighs

Laying patio block
Abdomen, shoulders, upper arms, forearms

Mixing and pouring concrete
Shoulders, abdomen, upper arms, forearms, hips and pelvis, thighs, lower legs

Mowing lawn (non-powered machine)
Shoulders, upper arms, forearms, abdomen, hips and pelvis, thighs, lower legs

Pruning shrubbery
Forearms, upper arms, shoulders, lower back

Raking grass or leaves
Shoulders, upper arms, forearms, abdomen, thighs, lower legs

Spading garden plot
Shoulders, abdomen, upper arms, forearms, hips and pelvis, thighs, lower legs

In many ways, the warming up and cooling down aspects of your exercise program are as important as the weight training itself. Here's a wide variety of activities designed to surround your body-building efforts.

Warming Up And Cooling Down

ATHLETES always warm up before a game or contest. At a baseball game, you can see the players warming up outside the dugout — stretching, bending, running. At a track and field meet, you can see racers jogging around the track while waiting to perform, or pole vaulters doing push-ups. These are not just idle activities. Athletes know that if they are to perform well, they must prepare their muscular, skeletal, and cardiovascular systems.

Books on running strongly advise joggers to warm up before a demanding run and to cool down after it. Any form of strenuous exercise — exercise that taxes your muscles, tendons, ligaments, heart, and lungs — should be preceded by well-planned warm-up exercises and followed by somewhat similar cooling off exercises.

Weight training is certainly a physical activity that requires pre- and post-exercise workouts. Because it is a vigorous exercise, body building places stress on the human body. In order to withstand such stress, muscles must be made loose and flexible, and blood must start pumping at an exercise level. Large amounts of oxygen must be taken into the body and carried by the bloodstream throughout the system. In short, you must get your body going before you start to lift weights.

In a similar fashion, you must taper off your exercise, not come to an abrupt halt. Runners usually jog a slow lap, competition swimmers take a last slow swim. This is the cool-down phase, a crucial link between vigorous activity and relative calm.

In many ways, the warming up and cooling down aspects of your exercise program are as important as the weight training itself. Therefore, you should plan to make these activities an integral part of your weight-training program. Because we don't want you to get bored with these exercises we are offering a wide variety from which you can choose. We suggest that you vary these exercises from session to session.

Warming Up

WARM-UP exercises are designed to work on the muscles, ligaments, tendons, and joints that will absorb the stress of the particular weight-training exercises that will follow. These warm-ups also exercise the heart and lungs, stimulating them and preparing them to meet more than their usual demands.

"Warming up" really means getting the oxygen-carrying blood flowing strongly to the muscles that will be exercised. There are two effective methods of warming up: loosening up calisthenics and light weight workouts. CONSUMER GUIDE® recommends that you do both prior to lifting. In a pinch one will do, but for a complete workout the two are recommended.

We do not specify a particular number of warm-up activities (such as 5 calisthenic exercises, for example). We do, however, recommend that you warm up regularly before you start any weight-training program, devoting a period of five to ten minutes to this phase of your workout. Feel free to pick and choose among the exercises. Be sure to correlate your warm-ups to the weight training that will follow — if your weight training will use the upper arm muscles, for example, make certain you warm up those muscles.

Calisthenics or light weight workouts — you can use either type, in any order, as warm-up activities. By mixing them up for the sake of variety, you can have a totally different warm-up session every time you exercise! It will be years before you start repeating a sequence.

Loosening-Up Calisthenics

FOLLOWING are 20 calisthenics and stretching exercises specially geared to prepare your joints for more vigorous exercise, loosen muscles and tendons, and generally prepare your body for more demanding activities. CONSUMER GUIDE® strongly suggests that you select 10 of these calisthenics and stretches prior to engaging in weight-training exercises.

Loosening-Up Calisthenics

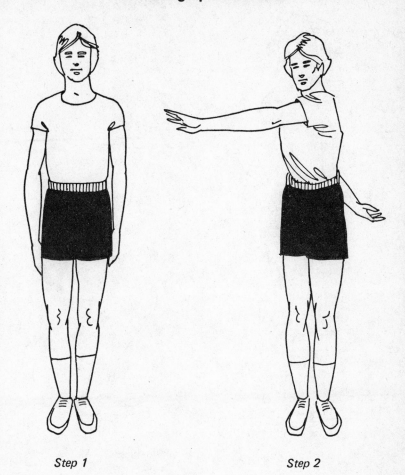

Step 1   Step 2

Trunk Twist
(to loosen the lateral abdominal muscles).
   1. Stand with feet together.
   2. Twist torso as far to the right as possible (without
   straining) allowing arms to swing.
   3. Twist it to the left in the same fashion.
   4. Repeat 10 to 20 times.

Loosening-Up Calisthenics

Step 2   *Step 3*

Modified Knee-Bend

(to warm up leg, thigh, and buttocks muscles).
1. Stand erect: shoulders squared, feet 6 to 12 inches apart.
2. Place hands on hips or extended out in front of body (whichever enables better balance).
3. Slowly lower body by bending the knees: stop at the half-squat position. Keep back straight.
4. Return to starting position.
5. Repeat 10 times.

Step 2

Calf Stretch
(to loosen calf muscles).
1. Stand in stride position: one foot forward, hands on hips.
2. Lean forward, bending advanced leg as much as possible, keeping heels of both feet on the floor.
3. Return to starting position.
4. Repeat with opposite leg forward.

Step 2

Stretch

(to stimulate muscles of waist, hips, groin, legs, and lower back).
  1. Squat on floor with buttocks on heels: body bent forward, hands on floor near knees for support.
  2. Extend one leg straight back as far as it will go, keeping back rigid.
  3. Press other knee toward the floor.
  4. Return to original position.
  5. Repeat exercise with opposite leg.
  6. Repeat full exercise 5 to 10 times.

Loosening-Up Calisthenics

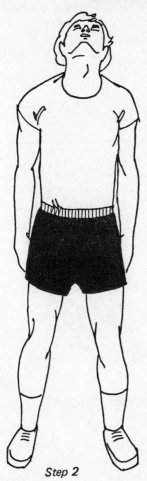

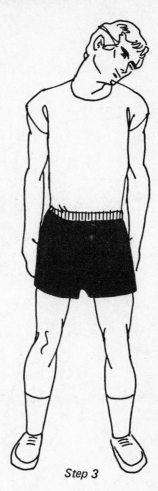

Step 2

Step 3

Neck Rotation
(to loosen neck muscles).
1. Stand with feet shoulder-width apart.
2. Bend head backward as far as it will go.
3. Turn head clockwise as far as it will go.
4. Return to starting position.
5. Repeat 10 to 20 times.
6. Repeat another 10 to 20 times rotating head in counterclockwise direction.

Loosening-Up Calisthenics

Step 1

Giant Arm Circles
(to loosen shoulder muscles).
1. Stand with feet together: arms extended at sides.
2. Make small clockwise circles with arms, gradually increasing circles to maximum size.

Loosening-Up Calisthenics

Step 2

3. Return to starting position.
4. Repeat approximately 20 times.
5. Repeat another 20 times with counterclockwise circles.

Loosening-Up Calisthenics

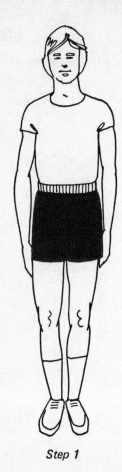

Step 1

Step 2

Side-Straddle-Hop
(to benefit respiration, leg muscles and lower back
muscles).
1. Stand erect: feet together, arms at sides, palms
   touching thighs.
2. Jump into a straddle position, simultaneously moving
   hands to clap together above the head.
3. Jump back to starting position, simultaneously
   lowering arms back to the sides.
4. Repeat 10 times.

Loosening-Up Calisthenics

Step 1

Step 2

Shoulder Roll

(to loosen any tightness in the shoulders).
1. Stand erect: arms at sides.
2. Move elbows out to the side horizontally, forming a 90-degree angle to body. Fingertips should touch shoulders.
3. Move elbows in a circular clockwise motion.
4. Repeat 20 times.
5. Repeat another 20 times in counterclockwise direction.

Loosening-Up Calisthenics

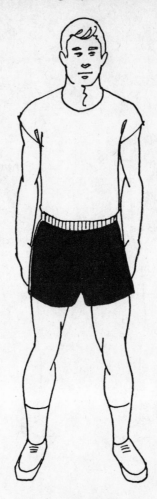

Step 1

Body Shakes
(to loosen muscles throughout the body).
   1. Stand with feet apart.
   2. Relax all muscles as loosely as possible.

Loosening-Up Calisthenics

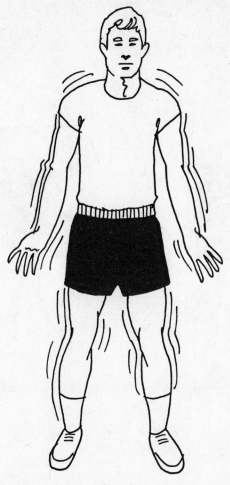

Step 3

3. Shake the entire body.
4. Take long, exaggerated steps.
5. Shake the arms, the legs, the trunk, and the neck.
6. Roll the head in a circle loosely.

Loosening-Up Calisthenics

Step 1

Step 2

Arm Pumps
(to loosen up biceps and triceps).
    1. Stand erect, feet shoulder-width apart, arms at sides.
    2. Pump arms back and forth approximately 20 times.

Stretching Exercise

Step 1

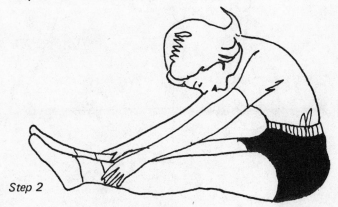

Step 2

Sitting Toe Touches
(to stretch leg and back muscles).
   1. Sit on floor: legs extended, feet together.
   2. Reach toward toes with both hands, bringing forehead
      as close to knees as possible.

Stretching Exercise

Step 2   *Step 5*

Calf Tendon Stretcher
(to loosen calf muscles).
1. Stand approximately 2 to 3 feet from the wall.
2. Lean forward, keeping body straight, place palms against the wall at eye level.
3. Step backward.
4. Continue to support weight with your hands.
5. Remain flat-footed until you feel calf muscles stretching.

Stretching Exercise

Step 1

Step 2

Calf Stretch
(to loosen calf muscles).
1. Stand in stride position: one foot forward, hands on hips.
2. Lean forward, bending advanced leg as much as possible, keeping heels of both feet on the floor.
3. Return to starting position.
4. Repeat with opposite leg forward.

Stretching Exercise

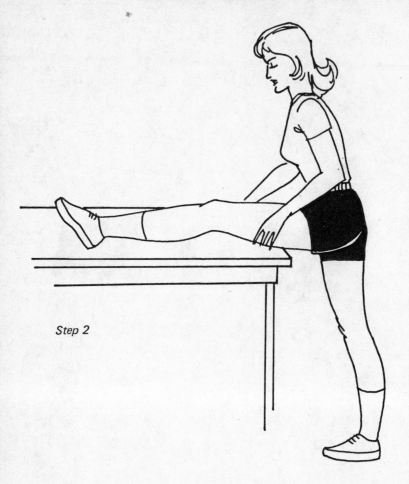

Step 2

Standing Leg Stretcher
(to loosen leg muscles).
    1. Use a chair or table approximately 3 feet in height.
    2. Place one foot on table so that knee is straight and leg
       is parallel to floor.

Stretching Exercise

Step 3

3. Slowly extend fingertips toward the outstretched leg. Try to touch forehead to knee.
4. Return to starting position.
5. Repeat exercise with other leg.

Stretching Exercise

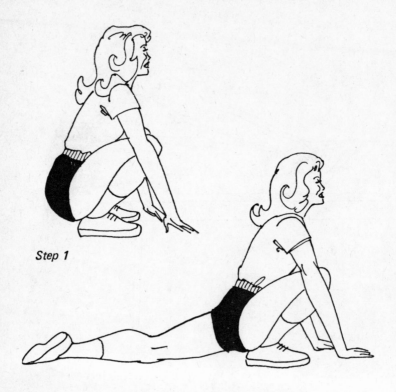

Step 1

Step 2

Sprinter
(to loosen leg muscles).
1. Assume squatting position: hands touching floor.
2. Extend one leg backward as far as possible.
3. Hold position for 5 to 10 seconds.
4. Return to starting position.
5. Repeat the entire exercise with other leg.

Stretching Exercise

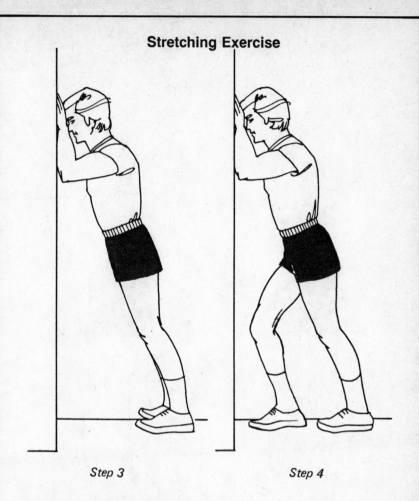

Step 3

Step 4

Calf/Achilles Stretch
(to stretch calf and Achilles tendon).
1. Stand facing a wall, 2 to 3 feet away.
2. Rest forearms on wall.
3. Place forehead on the back of hands.
4. Bend right knee and bring it half the distance toward the wall, keeping left leg straight, with heel on floor and toes pointed straight ahead.
5. Hold position 5 to 10 seconds. (You should feel the stretch in your calf.)
6. Return to starting position.
7. Repeat exercise with other leg.

Stretching Exercise

Step 2   *Step 3*

Side Stretch
(to loosen lateral muscles of the waist).
1. Stand with feet shoulder-width apart, legs straight.
2. Place one hand on hip, extend other arm up and over head.
3. Bend slowly toward the side of the hand on the hip. Move as far as you feel comfortable.
4. Hold the position for approximately 10 seconds.
5. Return to starting position.
6. Repeat exercise on other side.

Stretching Exercise

Step 2

Step 3

Shoulder Stretch
(to loosen shoulder muscles).
1. Stand erect with feet apart.
2. Place arms over head. Drop one hand over shoulder and down toward center of back.
3. With other hand, grasp bent elbow and push toward back; do not force it.
4. Hold elbow at its maximum (comfortable) 5 to 10 seconds.
5. Return to starting position.
6. Repeat opposite hand and elbow.

Stretching Exercise

Step 1

Step 4

Spinal Stretch
(to stretch and loosen muscles of the trunk).
1. Sit on floor: legs straight in front.
2. Keep right leg straight, place left foot on floor on the other side of right knee.
3. Reach over left leg with right arm so that elbow is on the outside of left leg.
4. Twist upper body to the left and place right elbow on outside of left knee.
5. Hold position 5 to 10 seconds.
6. Return to starting position.
7. Repeat exercise with other leg and elbow.

Stretching Exercise

Step 1

Step 2

Back Stretch
(to loosen back and leg muscles).
1. Stand erect: feet shoulder-width apart.
2. Bend forward slowly at waist.
3. Relax arms, shoulders, and neck.
4. Bend further — until you feel a slight stretch on the back of your legs. (If you cannot touch the floor, place your hands on the back of your legs. That will give you support.)
5. Hold this position for approximately 5 seconds. As you come back up, bend your knees to take the pressure off your lower back.

Light Weight Workouts

WARMING UP with lighter weights than you intend to use—performing the same exercises you will do with heavier weights — is the simplest of warm-up activities. We suggest that you use not more than half the weight you plan to use in the exercise and that you do no more than half the number of repetitions. You can, of course, individualize your efforts, as long as your workout is comfortable and free of strain. Remember, all you want to do is loosen up the muscles — the weight-training exercise comes later.

You do not have to warm up with exactly the same exercises. You should, however, select those that are fairly close to the kinds that you will be doing in the regular weight-training session.

Cooling Down, Tapering Off, Or Just Getting Back To Normal

AT THE END of a weight-training exercise period, give yourself some time to cool down, or taper off. Tapering off (as opposed to stopping physical activity suddenly) is just as important as warming up.

After completing a strenuous session of weight lifting, one of the worst things you can do is immediately lie or sit down to rest. You should keep your body in motion. Do some stretching exercises. Walk at a slow pace or run easily. Lift a light weight again. Do the body shakes. In other words, taper down slowly.

Abruptly stopping vigorous exercise can be dangerous because it leaves most of the blood in the wrong place. Sudden relaxation after a demanding session of lifting or other exercise could result in lightheadedness, dizziness, nausea, and even fainting or blackout. You have to let your body return to its normal state at a moderate rate. Cooling down or tapering off is a gradual slowing down from maximum (high) muscle contractions to minimum (low) muscle contractions.

When you are exercising vigorously, your heart is pumping blood through your arteries at a faster rate so that it can supply the active muscles with oxygen and life-supporting nutrients. The blood is forcefully pumped into the muscles by the contractions of the heart. There is, however, no similar force to send the blood back from the muscles to the heart by way of the veins. The veins carry the blood back toward the heart.

When you stop exercising suddenly, blood begins to pool in the muscles and veins. When you taper off, however, you avoid the delay in returning blood to the heart, thereby helping the body adjust to a condition of less activity. More blood is directed to the brain, lessening the danger of spasms and cramps in the muscles you have been exercising.

Tapering off also helps your body in another way. The fatigue from exercise creates a build-up of lactic acid in the muscles. Cooling off helps to dissipate the lactic acid and therefore eases muscle aches and pains. In addition, tapering off helps your body adjust to weather conditions outside the exercise area. It would be most unwise to go directly from a vigorous exercise session out into cold, wet weather.

If you are a beginner, don't be upset to discover that weight-training hampers your performance in other sports engaged in right after a workout. This happens because muscular tightness and fatigue often result from initial weight-training sessions. These problems, fortunately, are purely temporary conditions. Eventually, your muscles will become accustomed to the new demands placed on them.

One other negative factor regarding cool-down: Do not go into a sauna, a whirlpool bath, or a hot shower until you have cooled down completely. You know that you have cooled down when your heart beat has slowed and you have stopped sweating. Even then — when cool-down is complete — avoid the steam room. It will not rid you of aches and pains; it will not produce any permanent weight loss; and in some instances the steam room can actually pose a health hazard. A shower is fine — but only after some tapering off exercises. And then be sure to keep the water no hotter than lukewarm.

You can build a better body through weight training if you think of your program as a three-step process: (1) warm up, (2) work out, (3) cool down.

Weight training can provide you with a well-built, firm, and strong body, but it's not the only way to shape up. You can supplement your weight-lifting sessions with isometrics, dual-resistance exercises, and a host of calisthenics.

Extending The Program

THE BEST WAY to extend your efforts at building a better body is to incorporate a full cardiovascular exercise program. Weight training will provide you with a well-shaped, firm, and strong body, but it will not produce a fully fit circulatory and respiratory system. For that you need cardiovascular exercises — vigorous walking, running, bicycling, swimming, and cross-country skiing are a few of the best. Through a combination of weight training and cardiovascular exercise, you will create a better body both inside and out.

In addition to vigorous cardiovascular exercises, there are several other ways to supplement your weight-lifting activities. These supplements are simple and readily available to just about everyone. If you try to make everything you do an exercise, then there are virtually hundreds of ways in which you can augment your regular body-building routine. Learn to "think exercise." Here are some tips for converting everyday activities into useful exercise.

1. Always stand while dressing and undressing.
2. Park your car, or get off the bus or train, a few blocks from your destination. Walk the distance at a brisk rate.
3. Avoid using the elevator or escalator to go up or down two or three flights of stairs. If you must take the elevator, get off on the wrong floor and walk up two or three flights. You may find it invigorating to take two steps at a time.
4. Take a walk around the block in the morning and/or in the evening after work. If you have the time, take a walk after lunch.
5. After coming home from work, avoid dropping into a chair for the rest of the evening.
6. On your day off, wash the car yourself, get out and garden, rake leaves, or mow the lawn.
7. Stretch your muscles whenever possible while doing housework. Sweep and dust with brisk, vigorous movements.

Everyday Exercises

HERE ARE some additional exercises you can do to help get your body in shape between regular exercise sessions.

1. Pull in your abdomen when you are brushing your teeth, shaving, or talking on the telephone. Do not hold your breath. This maneuver is excellent for firming up your abdominal muscles.
2. While sitting, extend your legs and raise them. Hold them up for a few seconds, and then slowly lower them. This exercise will help the abdominal and thigh muscles.
3. When looking for a telephone number, twist your body to the side instead of placing the heavy phone book directly in front of you. This twisting movement will

exercise the muscles of the abdomen and the lower back.

4. Whenever possible, stretch to get something from a top shelf. This practice will add flexibility to the body.
5. When sitting in your chair, grasp the arms of the chair and push yourself slowly upward, then lower yourself back into the chair. Repeat this movement several times. Your arm and shoulder muscles will benefit from this exercise.
6. When you answer the telephone, grasp the handle tightly. The muscles of your hand and forearm will benefit from this grip-strengthening exercise.
7. Use desks, tables, or other suitable pieces of furniture as isometric devices. When sitting at a desk, push outward with your knees to either side of the desk well. Then place a small chair or sturdy wastebasket between your legs and push inward. Repeat this exercise several times. It will strengthen the thigh muscles.
8. Place your hands on top of your desk and push down firmly several times. Then place your hands under your desk and attempt to lift upward. These two exercises will strengthen the arm and shoulder muscles.
9. When you stand up, rise up on your toes and drop down on your heels several times. This exercise will add flexibility to the calf muscles.
10. When you sit down again at your desk, put your feet up on the desk and cross one leg over the other. In this position the legs are fully extended. Raise both legs and hold them up for a count of five. Then switch legs. The thigh and lower abdominal muscles will benefit.
11. Lean back against a wall and slide your body down, by bending at the knees, to a sitting position. Hold the position for 5 or 10 seconds. Your back and leg muscles will benefit.

Naturally, there will be times when you won't be able to exercise with weights. Few people tote barbells with them on vacation or business trips, and sometimes an injury or ailment can prevent a full-scale session of body building. During such times you may wish to draw upon three popular forms of exercise: isometric exercises, rope exercises and dual-resistance exercises.

Isometric Exercises

CONSUMER GUIDE® feels that isometric exercises have their strengths and limitations. It is our conclusion that:

1. Isometric exercises are to be considered a possible supplement to a complete fitness program. Under no circumstances should they be viewed as a total fitness program.
2. If isometric exercises are to be used as part of a fitness program, they should be viewed as a means of improving strength and increasing muscle definition or tone. It is recommended that the isometric exercises be supplemented with weight-training exercises and flexibility calisthenics. Aerobic-type exercises are also a must.
3. Flexibility and cardiovascular exercises are to be given priority over isometric exercises.
4. Even though the research is not absolutely conclusive, people suffering from heart disease or high blood pressure should not engage in these exercises unless given permission to do so by a physician knowledgeable in exercise and fitness.
5. Isometric exercises may be useful in improving strength in selected sports by simulating various positions used in the sport, i.e., a golf swing, tennis swing, etc.
6. Isometric exercises may be useful to people who must sit for extended periods of time.

A few of the more basic isometric exercises are described here. It should be understood that what follows is not a program of exercise but rather a sampling of the supplementary kinds of exercises you can perform to extend the CONSUMER GUIDE® body-building program.

In most instances a real maximum effort should be performed for six seconds. However, only exert about half effort until your body is in better condition.

Isometric Exercise

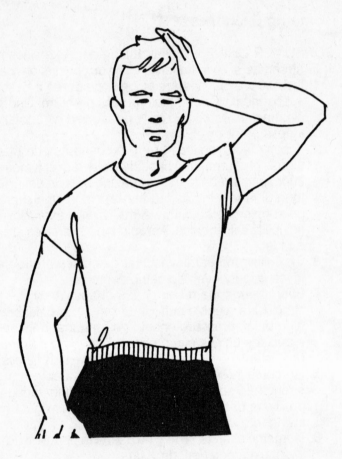

Step 1

Neck Press
(to strengthen the muscles of the neck and shoulders).
   1. Assume a standing position. Place the palm of the left
   hand against the left side of the head.
   2. Press with the head against the hand.
   3. Repeat on the right side, front, and back of head.

Isometric Exercise

Step 2

Doorway Press
(to strengthen the muscles of the shoulders, arms, upper back, and chest).
1. Stand in the center of a doorway, feet comfortably apart.
2. Place the hands against the doorway jambs so that the arms are extended upward above the head with palms against the jambs.
3. Press with both hands against the edges of the doorway. Be certain to keep the body straight.
Note: The exercise can also be modified to place the hands downward, at the sides and also placing the hands so that they are at shoulder-height with the arms bent.

Isometric Exercise

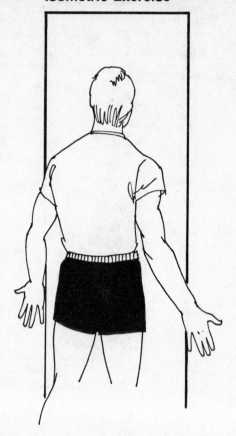

Step 2

Doorway Push
(to strengthen the muscles of the chest, shoulders, and arms).
1. Sit or stand in a doorway. Place hands at the sides of the body so they are at hip height.
2. Place palms on the outer borders of the doorway.
3. Press forward as though you were attempting to bring your arms forward so that the arms would meet in front of your body. Repeat exercise with hands on doorway at shoulder-height and again extended above the body.

Isometric Exercise

Step 2

Triceps Press
(to strengthen the muscles on the back of the arms).
1. Grasp a towel or rope with both hands.
2. Place right hand just above the right shoulder. Place left arm along the left side of your body with arm flexed so that your left hand is near the small of your back.
3. Attempt to extend both arms by trying to raise your right hand and lower your left.
4. Repeat reversing the above.

Isometric Exercise

Step 2

Arm Press
(to strengthen chest muscles and muscles at back of arms).
  1. Flex the arms and position the hands directly in front of the chest.
  2. Place the fist of one of the hands in the palm of the other.
  3. Push both hands against each other.

Isometric Exercise

Step 3

Forearm Press

(to develop muscles on the front and back of the arm and chest).

1. In a sitting or standing position, hold the right forearm across the body at chin level; bend your arm at the elbow so that the palm is facing upward.
2. Place the left hand on the wrist of the right hand.
3. Press upward with the right hand — resist with the left.
4. Repeat the exercise reversing arms.

Isometric Exercise

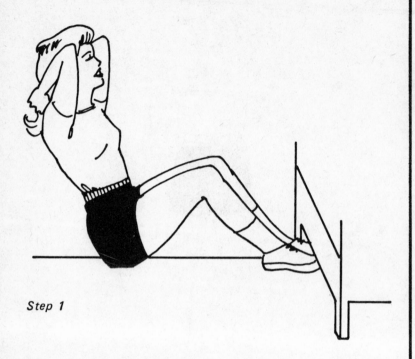

Step 1

Sit-Ups
(to strengthen the abdominal muscles).
1. With the feet placed under a chair, place the upper body at a 45-degree angle from the floor.
2. Extend the arms in front of the body. Hold that position for 10 to 20 seconds. If you cannot maintain the postion, move the upper body to reduce the stress.
Note: To make the exercise more difficult, lock the hands in back of the head.

Step 2

Stomach Pull
(to strengthen the abdominal muscles).
1. Assume a standing, sitting, or lying position.
2. Exhale and then contract the abdominal muscles as
   though trying to push the muscles to the backbone.

Isometric Exercise

Step 1

Step 2

Abdominal Curl
(to strengthen the abdomen).
    1. Assume a supine position with the arms at the sides.
    2. Bend knees and attempt to curl upward and forward, while keeping the lower back on the floor.

Step 3

One-Leg Squat

(to strengthen the knee and the muscles on the front of the thigh).

1. Assume a standing position next to a wall and extend the left leg forward.
2. Squat with the right leg until the upper leg and lower leg form a 90-degree angle.
3. Place your hand against the wall, if necessary to maintain balance. Hold this position without bending the trunk.
4. Reverse with the other leg.

Isometric Exercise

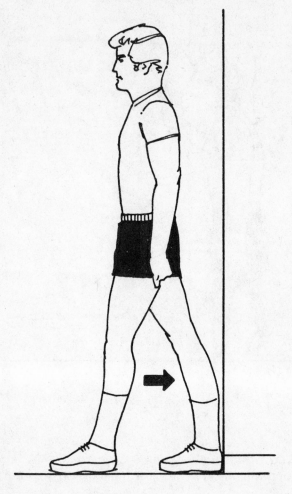

Step 3

Leg Wall Push
(to strengthen the muscles at the back of the upper leg).
1. Stand about 18 inches from the wall, with your back toward it.
2. Place your right foot backward so that your heel touches the wall.
3. Push backward with your heel that is against the wall.
4. Repeat with other leg.

Getting Fit With A Rope

A ROPE can be used for some isometric exercises. You can put the rope in your suitcase or attache case and continue your body-building program while traveling.

Although you can purchase a specially made rope, our suggestion is to design your own. Get a 10 foot length of stretch-resistant polypropylene and tie it together with a square knot. You might also place two plastic handles on the rope before tying the rope together. This will provide maximum comfort and convenience when carrying out the various exercises. If this is not possible, wear gloves to protect your hands.

The isometric exercise program that CONSUMER GUIDE® describes on the following pages is a simple program to supplement your weight-training program. It is designed to be used when weights are not available. But when undertaking the rope isometric program, follow these safety precautions.

1. Before doing the exercises make sure you do the loosening-up calisthenics. These will prepare your muscles and joints for more vigorous activity.
2. During the first two weeks that you do these exercises with the rope, we suggest that you hold for no longer than three seconds. It's a good idea to gradually contract the muscles slowly and then exert an almost maximum effort for three seconds.
3. After the three second hard effort, relax. Shake your arms and legs.
4. As your condition improves you can gradually increase your contractions toward six to nine seconds.
5. Wear hard-soled shoes since the rope can dig into the sides of your feet.
6. Don't forget the rubber grips on the rope to help protect the hands, or wear gloves.

Following are a series of rope exercises that you can do while on the road.

Rope Exercise

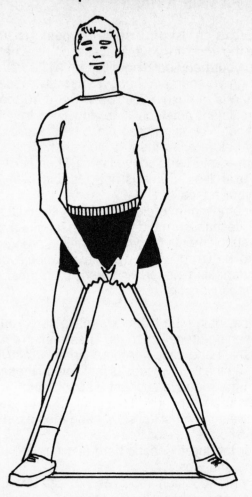

Step 2

Giant Pull

(to strengthen your shoulder, arm, chest, and upper back muscles).

1. Place the rope under your feet and spread them comfortably. Position your feet about six inches wider than shoulder-width apart.
2. Grasp the rope with your palms in toward the body. Keep your legs straight, back straight, and head up.
3. Exert a pull upward with your arms bent at the elbow.

Rope Exercise

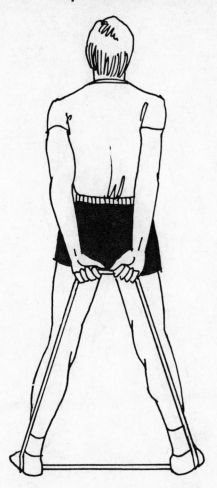

Step 2

Back Pull
(to strengthen your arm, shoulder, and upper back muscles).
1. Place the rope under your feet.
2. Place your hands together behind your back and grasp the rope with your palms turned outward.
3. Spread your feet about six inches wider than shoulder-width apart.
4. Keeping your arms straight, pull upward and forward with your shoulders. Do not bend your arms or hips.

Rope Exercise

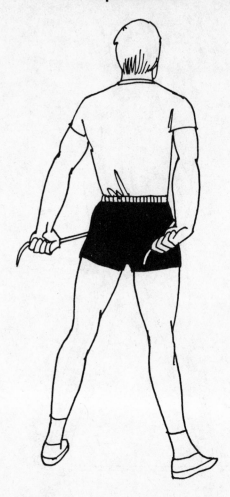

Step 3

Backward Pull
(to strengthen your upper back and muscles at the back of the arm).
1. Grasp the rope and place it across your body in front of you.
2. The arms should be hanging at your sides and the palms of your hands should be turned backward.
3. Keeping your arms straight, exert a force backward and upward.

Rope Exercise

Step 1

Backward Raise
(to strengthen the muscles which cap your shoulders, your triceps, and your forearm muscles).
1. Loop the rope twice and place it behind your back.
2. With the palms of your hands turned in toward your thighs, grasp the rope and exert a pull outward and away from your body.

Rope Exercise

Step 2

Curl
(to strengthen the muscle on the front of the arm).
1. Place the rope behind your body and position it under your buttocks.
2. Grasp the rope with the palms of your hands turned upward.
3. Keeping your elbows pressed against your sides, with your arms bent at a 90-degree angle, exert a force upward.

Rope Exercise

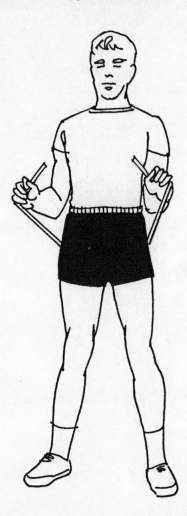

Step 2

Reverse Curl
(to strengthen the muscle on the front of the arm).
1. Place the rope behind your back and position it under your buttocks much like you did in the Curl exercise.
2. Grasp the rope with your palms turned downward.
3. Spread your hands wider than your shoulders.
4. Keep your elbows away from your body and exert a pull upward and outward and slightly to the back.

Rope Exercise

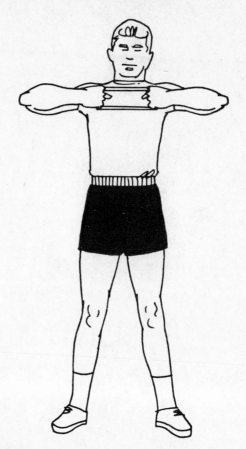

Step 2

Charlie Atlas

(to strengthen muscles of the upper body, chest, and arms).

1. Loop the rope twice.
2. Place it in front of your chest and grasp the rope with the palms of your hands turned in toward your body.
3. Keeping your hands as close to your chest as possible, pull outward with your arms and maintain a contraction.
   Two variations are to loop the rope once and perform the exercise. And then have the rope in its normal position and do the exercise.

Rope Exercise

Step 1

Arm Extender
(to strengthen the muscle which caps the shoulder, the triceps, and the muscles of the forearm).
1. Grasp the rope and hold it in front of your body with your arms extended outward.
2. The palms of your hands should be turned outward.
3. Exert a pull outward and in a direction parallel to the floor.

Rope Exercise

Step 2

Leg Strengtheners
(to strengthen the muscles in the back of the leg).
   1. Loop the rope and place it around your ankles.
   2. Keeping both legs straight, exert pressure backward
       with one leg.
   3. Repeat the exercise with the other leg.

Rope Exercise

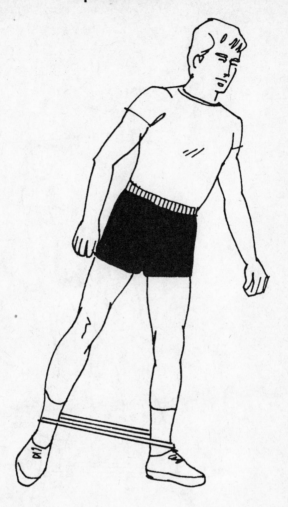

Step 2

Leg Abductor
(to strengthen the muscles at the front of the leg and also the abductor muscles).
1. Loop the rope and place it around the ankles.
2. While standing on one leg, raise the other leg sidewards.
3. Maintain that position.
4. Reverse the position and repeat with the other leg.

Rope Exercise

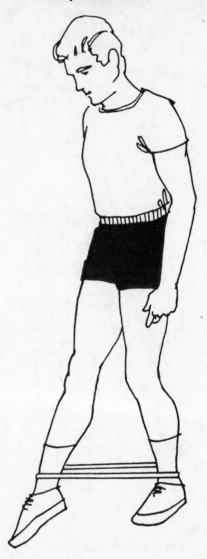

Step 2

Quad Setter
(to strengthen the muscles on the front of the leg).
1. Loop the rope and place it around the ankles.
2. Extend one foot forward while keeping your knees straight and exert a force.
3. Repeat with other leg.

The neat thing about the rope is that you can also use it for rope jumping. Rope jumping is an excellent supplementary exercise and extremely popular today. If you wish, simply take the rope you used for isometrics and untie the square knot. If the rope seems a little long you can simply wrap the ends around your hands. (The rope should be long enough so that you can stand on it and pull the rope up to your armpits.)

Rope jumping helps improve muscle tone, strength, flexibility and agility. It also provides a little fun in the process. Many physical fitness authorities believe that regular, vigorous rope jumping is at least as beneficial as jogging.

You can jump rope almost anywhere. All you need is enough space to swing the rope. And wherever you go, you can take your jump rope with you. It curls up handily into a briefcase or large purse. It is an amazingly effective device for relieving boredom and getting good muscle toning and cardiovascular exercise at the same time. Jumping rope for a few minutes just before every meal can also help reduce your appetite.

Some of you may feel that a jump rope made especially for exercise purposes is best. With good equipment, you will achieve your best performance. A professional molded leather jump rope has wooden handles and heavy ball bearings for easy turning. It comes in one standard length — 118 inches (including the handles). If the rope is too long for you, tie one or more knots in it.

Always wear shoes when you jump. If you go barefoot, the rope may get caught in the toe — and that can be very painful. Wear running shoes.

You can wear anything comfortable and loose that doesn't bind at the crotch — shorts or slacks will do. Women should wear a bra because of the whip-like action of the chest on the muscles that support the breasts.

Bear in mind before you start to jump rope that it is a very strenuous exercise. Treat jumping rope as you would a running program, consulting your physician before launching into it. Work by the clock when jumping rope. Your ultimate goal is to aim for around 15 to 20 minutes at a time. You will undoubtedly have to work your way up to that figure. It is CONSUMER GUIDE®'s opinion that you try jumping for one minute, resting a minute and then jumping another minute. That's all the first day. Then every three days or so add another minute of exercise and a minute of rest. For some people it may take a week to add a full minute. You will have to be your own judge. After you are jumping 8 minutes and resting 7, jump 2 minutes with a rest of one minute. Then gradually increase your exercise time and reduce your resting time. Follow this pattern until you are able to jump 15 to 20 minutes non stop.

And as far as the jumping technique is concerned, land on the balls of your feet rather than flat-footed. Jump as lightly as possible (like a dancer). Try not to pound your feet into the floor. Turn the rope from the wrists. If you get too much arm action you will get tired before you've finished your session.

When you do get tired, regardless of the time that you've set up, stop for a while. This is especially important when you're just beginning to jump rope. You're supposed to enjoy it, not feel that you're being destroyed by a length of rope or leather. When you do stop, drop your rope, and walk around the room shaking your arms and legs. You might also try to stretch your calf muscles with the Calf Achilles Stretch.

Dual - Resistance Exercises

THERE ARE a host of exercises you can do with someone else to build a better body. Called dual-resistance exercises, they are fun and recreational as well as a proven method for developing overall muscular strength and improving muscle tone and appearance. They are also good for toning specific areas of your body.

As the name implies, dual-resistance exercises mean two people exercise together. One supplies the resistance, while the other does the exercise. No equipment is necessary; neither are any special areas or special types of facilities. Your family room, basement, or even the bedroom is perfect. All you need are a few simple exercises to start, since you will come up with your own dual-resistance exercises after a few sessions.

The best way to explain how to do these partner exercises is to take you through a step-by-step description of one of the exercises — the Forearm Curl. You and your partner stand facing one another. Your partner stands with his arms against his sides and with the palms of his hands facing forward and upward. You then place your fists in his open hands. While keeping his upper arms against his sides, he forcefully raises his hands through an arc and toward his shoulders. While he is doing that, you simply supply sufficient resistance to allow movement to proceed slowly throughout the range of motion. When your partner's hands touch his shoulders, you slowly begin to force them down to the starting position. Repeat this same movement several times and then change roles.

It's just that simple. You will be amazed at how quickly your strength will build up after a few weeks of dual-resistance exercise. All the dual-resistance exercises follow these same principles, only the starting positions, holds, and body areas affected are different.

The Forearm Curl described is an example of the isotonic exercise done in much the same manner as in weight-training exercises. The only difference is that the resister takes the place of the barbells. Trying to lift your arms to touch your shoulders while the other person pushes down produces the same effect as if you were trying to raise a barbell toward your chest. The resistance offered by the resister should be such that 8 to 10 seconds are required for the exerciser to complete the full range of motion.

There is still another type of workout that you can get with dual-resistance exercises. Instead of allowing your partner to curl up the arms in the Forearm Curl, you can supply enough resistance so that he cannot move his arms. When that happens, you are doing isometrics. By interchanging isotonic and isometric exercise you can go a long way toward keeping interest high.

The exercises listed here are categorized according to the area of the body they benefit. When you're deciding which ones to include, choose a variety in order to strengthen all parts of your body. Do at least three repetitions of each exercise, and then change roles with your partner and do three more.

Dual-Resistance
Exercise For The Shoulders

Step 1

Elbow Push-Down

1. Ready Position: Face your partner. Bend your elbows, hands in front of shoulders with your elbows pointing toward him. Your partner places the palms of his hands under your elbows.

2. Isotonic Action: Force your elbows downward toward the sides of your body. When the elbows are next to the body, your partner should force your elbows back to the original position.

3. Isometric Action: Attempt to force your elbows downward toward the sides of your body, while your partner resists and does not permit movement.

Dual-Resistance
Exercise For The Shoulders

Step 1

Supine Press

1. Ready Position: Assume a reclining position with knees bent, on the floor or mat with your arms flexed and elbows against your sides. Hold your hands, palms up, near your shoulders. Your partner should kneel behind you and lean forward, grasping your hands.

2. Isotonic Action: Slowly force your hands upward until your arms are completely extended. Be sure to keep your hands directly above your shoulders. Once arms are completely extended, your partner should force your hands back to the starting position.

3. Isometric Action: Attempt to force your hands upward, while your partner actively resists so that no movement takes place.

Dual-Resistance
Exercise For The Shoulders

Step 1

Supine Pull Over
1. Ready position: Assume a reclining position with your knees bent and your arms extended over your head. Your partner assumes a kneeling position behind your head and then grasps your forearms.
2. Isotonic Action: Move your arms upward to a vertical position. Keep the elbows locked throughout the movement.
3. Isometric Action: Attempt to move your arms upward to a vertical position, while your partner prohibits any movement. This exercise is a perfect example of how you can place the arms in various positions so that the muscle groups are exercised in their full range of motion.

Dual-Resistance
Exercise For The Shoulders

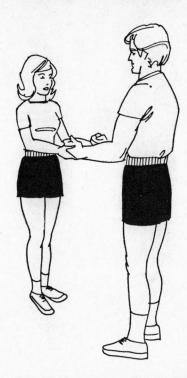

Step 3

Forearm Curl

1. **Ready Position:** Face your partner. Stand with your arms against your sides with the palms facing forward and upward. Your partner places his fist in your open palms or against your wrists.
2. **Isotonic Action:** Forcibly raise your forearms to your shoulders, being certain that your upper arms are against the sides of your body as the movement is made. As soon as your partner's hands touch your shoulders, he should force your hands back down to the starting position.
3. **Isometric Action:** Place your forearms at waist height — upper arms and lower arms form right angles. Attempt to raise your forearms while your partner actively resists and permits no movement.

Dual-Resistance
Exercise For The Arms

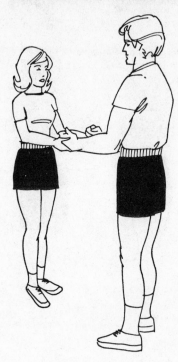

Step 3

Reverse Curl

1. Ready Position: In this variation of the forearm curl, take the same position as for the Forearm Curl except face your palms toward the floor as your partner grasps the backs of your hands or wrists.

2. Isotonic Action: Forcibly raise your forearms to your shoulders, being certain that your upper arms are against the sides of your body as the movement is made. As soon as your partner's hands touch your shoulders, he should force your hands back down to the starting position.

3. Isometric Action: Place your forearms at waist height — upper arms and lower arms form right angles. Attempt to raise your forearms while your partner actively resists and permits no movement.

Dual-Resistance
Exercise For The Arms

Step 2

Resistance Push-Up
1. Ready Position: Assume a push-up position with elbows bent at a 90-degree angle. Your partner straddles your hips and places his hands on your shoulder blades.
2. Isotonic Action: Execute a push-up until your arms are extended while your partner slows your movement. When your arms are extended, your partner pushes you back to the starting position.
3. Isometric Action: Attempt to straighten your arms as you would in a push-up while your partner resists.

Dual-Resistance
Exercise For The Abdomen

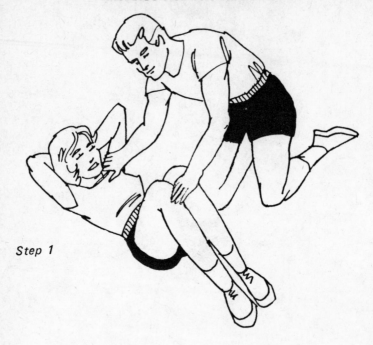

Step 1

Bent Leg Sit-Up
1. Ready Position: In a supine position bend the knees so that your heels are drawn up near your buttocks. Lock your fingers behind your head. Your partner kneels next to you with one hand on your chest and the other hand on your knees.
2. Isotonic Action: Slowly curl your upper body until the trunk comes to an erect position. Then your partner slowly forces you into the starting position.
3. Isometric Action: Assume an upright position. Resist as your partner attempts to push you down to a supine position. A variation is to attempt a sit-up as your partner resists. Or you can assume a 45-degree angle as your partner attempts to push you down.

Dual-Resistance
Exercise For The Abdomen

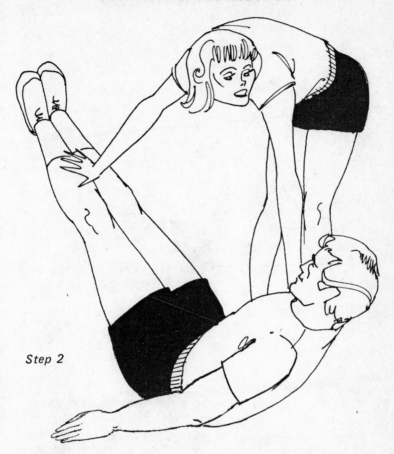

Step 2

V-Sit-Up
1. **Ready Position:** Lie down, raise legs and upper body simultaneously, keeping the legs straight and arms out straight for balance. Your partner stands beside you and places his one hand on your chest and his other hand on your shin or calf.
2. **Isotonic Action:** Your partner slowly pushes your back and legs to the floor. Then you slowly raise both legs and back off the floor to the starting position.
3. **Isometric Action:** Your partner attempts to push your back and legs to the floor while you resist.

Dual-Resistance
Exercise For The Abdomen

Step 2

Lateral Sit-Up

1. Ready Position: Assume a right-side lying position, with left arm across your chest with palm of left hand on floor. Extend right arm above head on floor. The resister sits straddling your thighs, with both hands on your left shoulder.

2. Isotonic Action: Raise your upper body off the floor laterally as high as possible. When this point is reached, the resister slowly pushes you down to the ground, after which you return to the side upright position. After the three or four sets are completed, you should be on the left side.

3. Isometric Action: Raise your upper body off the floor laterally or as high as possible. The resister attempts to push you down. The exercise must be performed on both sides.

Dual-Resistance
Exercise For The Hips And Legs

Step 1

Side Leg Raising

1. **Ready Position:** Assume a right-side lying position, and bend the right leg slightly for stability. Place the left hand across the chest. Your partner stands behind you and places one hand on your shoulder and the other on your ankle.
2. **Isotonic Action:** Raise your top leg as high as possible, without bending the knee. Your partner slows the movement. When your leg is raised as high as possible, he pushes the leg back to the starting position. Perform the exercise on both sides.
3. **Isometric Action:** Raise your leg to little less than a 45-degree angle, and rotate it inward slightly. Your partner attempts to push the leg downward while you resist.

Dual-Resistance
Exercise For The Hips And Legs

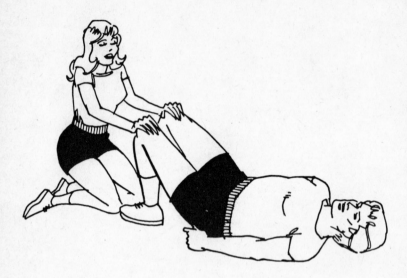

Step 1

Hip Adduction (Hips and Knees Bent)

1. **Ready Position:** Assume a supine position with your knees bent and feet flat on the floor. Put your arms beside your body. Your partner kneels next to your feet and places one hand on each of your knees.
2. **Isotonic Action:** Slowly pull the two knees apart while your partner resists. Once the knees are pulled apart, slowly close them as your partner resists.
3. **Isometric Action:** Open your knees slightly in the ready position. Your partner attempts to push open the legs while you resist.

Dual-Resistance
Exercise For The Hips And Legs

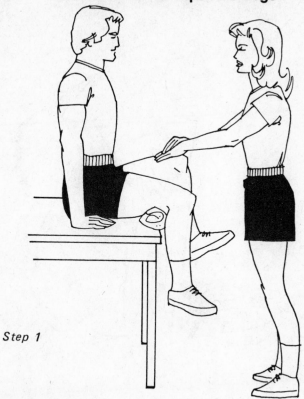

Step 1

Knee Bent Flexion
1. Ready Position: Sit on a table with a towel rolled under your knees for comfort. Place your hands on the outside of the knees for stability. Your partner stands in front of your legs and clasps both hands on top of one of your knees.
2. Isotonic Action: Slowly raise the resisted knee toward the ceiling, being certain that the knee is kept bent. Once the knee reaches its maximum height, your partner slowly pushes the leg back to the table. Exercise both legs.
3. Isometric Action: Attempt to raise the knee while your partner resists that movement. A variation is to start the knee at the point of maximum height.

Dual-Resistance
Exercise For The Hips And Legs

Step 3

Leg Curl

1. **Ready Position:** Lie in a prone position with your legs together. Your partner kneels beside your thighs, placing his one hand on your ankle and the other on your back thigh.
2. **Isotonic Action:** Slowly curl your lower leg upward while your thigh is held down. When the lower leg is curled as far as possible, your partner slowly pushes your leg back to the starting position. Exercise both legs.
3. **Isometric Action:** Partially curl your leg. First your partner attempts to push the leg to the upper thigh as you resist. Then, with your leg at a half-curl position, he attempts to push the leg back to the prone position.

Like everyone who exercises
regularly and strenuously,
people who work out with
weights can suffer a variety of
aches and pains. Learn how
to treat minor hurts and to
recognize signs of possible
danger.

Hurts And What To Do About Them

TO BE a good weight trainer, you have to learn to listen to your body. Most of the serious injuries, aches, pains experienced by people who work out regularly could be prevented. Precaution is the key word. If you use well-maintained equipment of good quality, prepare yourself before the physical activity and cool down afterwards, and listen to your body, you can avoid most injuries or ailments.

Despite the best precautions, however, people who exercise strenuously can encounter some aches and pains regularly. Weight trainers are no exception. Aside from injuries caused by a cast-iron barbell or dumbbell falling on a foot, there are a host of other pains that can plague the person who works out with weights. In this chapter we will present some generalized guidelines for helping you avoid potential injury. We will also look at specific types of discomfort that you could encounter and offer some advice and guidance for dealing with them.

Some General Rules

WHEN YOU first start any exercise program — calisthenics, running, or weight training — you can expect to experience various aches and pains. Certain muscles will become stiff and sore because you are making new demands on them. Normally, though, the soreness and stiffness will fade away. What you have to watch out for are the painful injuries that do not fade away so easily.

For anybody embarking on a program of exercise, the watchwords are: "Train, don't strain." Be conscious of and practice safety at all times, and adhere strictly to the proper techniques described with each exercise in the CONSUMER GUIDE® program. If you do in fact train without strain, you will prevent most of the injuries or problems discussed in this chapter. In order to help you, we have devised a "Hurt-Free Checklist." Follow its suggestions and you will minimize the possibilities of long-lasting pain and injury.

Hurt-Free Checklist

Mental Attitude — Are you feeling "up" and ready to exercise today? Or are you just going to drag through them? Will exercise improve your mental attitude?

Warming Up — Have you warmed up properly? Are you taking enough time (at least 5 to 10 minutes) to loosen your muscles and improve your flexibility before you start the lifting exercises?

Clothing — Does your clothing fit well, not too tight and not too loose? It is advisable for both men and women to wear a top with sleeves; sleeveless tops can permit a too-rapid rate of muscle cooling.

Equipment Check — Did you select the proper weights

and equipment for the specific exercise you plan to do? Are the weights locked securely in place on the barbell, with collars in front and behind? Are other weights and equipment out of the way so that they do not hinder your particular exercise?

Equipment Handling — Are you showing sufficient respect for the weights? Do you always make certain that your grip is firm and secure? Are you trying to change your grip in midair? Have you forgotten that the proper method for grip changing is to set the barbell down carefully, change your grip, and start over again?

Lifting — Are you lifting properly, putting stress on the legs rather than on the back? Are you cheating on any lift, cutting corners to make it easier?

Breathing — Are you breathing deeply and regularly during the lift?

Fatigue — Do you consistently stop lifting before you become exhausted? Do you fall into that just-one-more lift syndrome? Most athletic accidents happen because the competitor has over-extended himself or herself. Training to the point of exhaustion does not increase endurance.

Competition — Do you try to compete with the power lifters in the gym? Are you content staying with your own body-building program at your own rate?

Tapering Off — Are you cooling down gradually and comfortably, remembering that tapering off is important to your heart and the rest of your cardiovascular system? Do you cool off and wind down before you take a shower or go out into cold weather?

Persistent Pain — Are you listening to your body? Do you attempt to fool yourself into thinking that persistent pain in a particular part of the body will go away? Do you consult a physician about long-lasting pain?

Physical Condition — Are you continuing strenuous exercise when you have a cold, flu, or other internal ailment? Are you working on a muscle or muscle group that is injured or one that should be rested?

The Nuisances

THE HURTS discussed below — better termed "nuisances" — are often unavoidable, but they are sometimes incurred due to carelessness. Although uncomfortable, they offer little to worry about. If any of these pains persist, however, they should no longer be regarded simply as nuisances, and a physician should be consulted. In most cases, though, nuisance ailments will go away with little or no treatment.

Muscle Stiffness And Soreness

STIFFNESS and soreness of muscles can be expected during the initial stages of any relatively rigorous exercise program. The CONSUMER GUIDE® program is no exception. In the beginning you will feel the effects of your efforts, and this soreness and stiffness will recur from time to time as you try new exercises or lifts.

Muscles get sore when they are not conditioned to being used. When muscles are called upon for unusual activity, the waste products — lactic acid and carbon dioxide — pile up in the muscle cells faster than the blood can carry them away. These surplus waste products stimulate pain receptors, which send messages of "stiff" and "sore" to the brain. As the circulatory system becomes more efficient, stiffness and soreness will become less noticeable and eventually disappear.

Muscle soreness and stiffness can also be caused by the tearing of muscle fiber during strenuous activity. This particular type of soreness may not appear at once — perhaps not until several days have passed. It is a form of muscle soreness that usually persists a while and should be checked out by a physician or professional therapist.

To minimize the problem of stiff and sore muscles, plan your conditioning program to progress slowly and gradually, especially during the early stages. Take rest periods when you feel you need them, and rest for as long as you need. A mature athlete is willing to take time out when he or she feels overheated or fatigued. Many of us do not respect our body's messages: we want to keep going to satisfy our egos, but such ego fulfillment is foolish and potentially hazardous.

Muscle soreness can be alleviated by extending the length of time devoted to warming up and tapering off. After cooling off, gently contract and relax any sore muscles a few times. If soreness is severe, apply ice packs to slow down the blood flow and help to prevent any possible internal bleeding or muscle hemorrhage. With severe soreness, be certain to consult a doctor.

Blisters

RUNNERS have problems with blisters on their feet. Weight lifters have problems with blisters on their hands, although they frequently experience foot blisters as well. Blisters occur when pressure is continually exerted on a particular part of the body during physical activity. If the pressure creates a chafing or rubbing effect, one or more blisters are likely to appear.

Always resist the temptation to lance or puncture an unbroken blister. Instead, wash the blister gently with soap and water, and then cover it with an adhesive compress. Leave the blister alone until the fluids in it are absorbed back into the body naturally.

If the blister is large, it may very well burst without your doing anything at all. If it appears about to burst, you can rupture it carefully and antiseptically. Sterilize a needle by holding it in a flame, and then puncture the blister at two separate points with the sterilized needle. Gently press the blister with sterile gauze to force out the fluid. Then disinfect the open sore with an antiseptic, and cover it with a sterile dressing or adhesive bandage.

If the blistered skin has been rubbed off, exposing a raw surface, clean the area with warm soapy water and apply an antiseptic. Cover the area with a sterile dressing.

If there are any signs that the blister is becoming red or

otherwise noticeably discolored, or that it is secreting puss-like fluids, it has probably become infected. If so, have your doctor look at it immediately; any infection can be dangerous. If you want to continue to lift even though you have a blister, make a small gauze pad for your hand to protect the blister.

A little foot powder sprinkled into your shoes will often help to prevent foot blisters. If foot blisters persist, you may have poorly fitted shoes. Check your fit at a reliable shoe store, and buy a new pair if necessary. Since sock thickness can have a bearing on proper shoe size, be sure to wear the socks you would normally wear for exercise when you have your present shoes checked and/or when you buy a new pair.

Muscle Cramps

AN INVOLUNTARY, powerful, painful contraction of a muscle means that you have a muscle cramp. Muscle cramps occur in both active and sedentary people. No one knows for sure what causes them, but it is generally agreed that unaccustomed exercise will increase the chances of getting muscle cramps.

The constricting pain of a muscle cramp can strike at any time: while lifting weights, doing calisthenics, running, working at a desk, resting, or even when sleeping. These cramps usually strike without warning, although occasionally there are indications that a cramp is coming.

Stretching the tightened-up muscle is the cure for the pain. If the muscle cramp is in your leg, for example, get to your feet immediately and walk on the leg, no matter how painful it may be. After you have taken a few steps, the muscle should begin to relax and the pain diminish. After the cramp is gone, rest the leg.

For muscle cramps in any part of the body, it is helpful to apply thumb pressure at the center of the cramped muscle. Slowly stretch the muscle within the normal range of motion. With your thumb, massage gently to reduce spasm. If the pain continues, apply moist heat (hot compresses). When you can get the muscle relaxed and rested, gently work it several times until it feels normal again.

A few simple precautions can reduce your chances of getting cramped muscles during body-building exercises. When you feel yourself getting tired, relax your tense muscles and rest. Don't try for that extra lift or that extra set of exercises. If your clothing is cutting off circulation, loosen it. The better shape you are in, the lesser the likelihood you will suffer muscle cramps — although it should be pointed out that some people are simply more liable to cramping than others.

Scratches, Scrapes, And Skinnings

SCRATCHES, scrapes and mat or floor burns are occupational hazards of weight training. These nuisances may look unimportant, and you may be tempted to ignore them; but they could develop into problems.

Be especially wary of scratches and scrapes caused by rusty or dirty objects. The spores of tetanus, or lockjaw, may be present and enter the body through even the most trivial wound. Wash all cuts and abrasions with soap and water. If you have not had a recent tetanus inoculation, get one. If you have an allergic reaction to the horse serum from which tetanus antitoxin is usually made, you can ask for antitoxin prepared from human donors. Active, long-term immunity to tetanus can be easily achieved by immunization.

If infection sets in after any scratch, scrape, or skinning, see a physician immediately.

Strained Muscles Or Tendons

STRAINS caused by overstretching are usually referred to as "pulled muscles" or "pulled tendons." A sharp pain or "stitch" at the moment of the injury is evidence of a pulled muscle or tendon. Runners come up suddenly lame when they have pulled a muscle in the leg and they frequently experience worsening stiffness and soreness for two or three hours.

Moving the area affected by a strained muscle or tendon is quite painful, and the best treatment involves sitting or lying in the most comfortable position. Apply heat in any convenient form (heat lamp, hot water bottle, electric heating pad, etc.), and gently massage the painful area with warm rubbing alcohol or witch hazel.

When the soreness begins to leave you can resume exercise, but you should do so cautiously, a little at a time. Most pulled muscles will not require anything more for healing than rest and a little patience on your part.

More Serious Hurts

WORKING with weights involves most of the crucial body parts: the heart, lungs, spine, legs, and arms. As a consequence, it is possible to injure one or more of these crucial parts through overexertion or accident. By the same token, most accidents or injuries can be avoided with a bit of common sense and caution.

Always stop exercising if you experience dizziness, abnormal pain or tightness in the chest, light-headedness, unnatural breathlessness, loss of muscle control, double vision or abnormal sight problems, nausea, chills, or cold sweats. Stop also if you sense injury to a muscle, tendon, or joint. The problem may be just of the nuisance variety, but it can develop into a serious injury if treated imprudently.

Here are some potentially serious injuries or symptoms. Some require consultation with a physician, but most represent temporary problems that seldom prevent anyone from resuming an exercise program after sufficient rest and treatment.

Lower Back Strain

LOWER BACK strain most often results from improper lifting or from trying to lift objects that are too heavy. It is a common complaint of the beginning weight lifter who rushes into a program inadequately prepared. It is also common among people who stoop from the waist instead of bending at the knees in order to lift boxes, bundles, boulders, or other heavy objects.

The results of careless lifting or overstraining are not always apparent immediately. You might lift a large sack of yard refuse by bending over instead of squatting. You might then feel fine for a couple of days. But soon afterwards you may be unable to straighten up!

Never let the lower back arch forward when you are lifting weights (or any heavy object), and never bend over stiff-legged to lift. Your back can't handle this kind of stress. Always use the proper weight-lifting technique for the exercise, and consciously use your leg muscles rather than your back muscles when lifting heavy items around the house.

Many doctors believe that the first onset of relatively mild lower back pain is a sign for the patient to take more active exercise. Adequate regular exercise of the muscles of the abdomen will strengthen these muscles for the jobs that they have to do (such as keeping us erect and holding the organs of the abdomen in place) and will improve their tone and balance. Exercises to stretch the lower back are also important. Such exercises should also help to correct faults in posture which may aggravate lower back strain.

If lower back pain persists, see your doctor. He or she may well prescribe some therapeutic lifts to help you work your way out of lower back pain. The doctor may also recommend that you sleep on a firm mattress placed over a bedboard.

Shoulder Strain

SHOULDER strain is one of the most common injuries associated with weight training. The deltoid muscle — the muscle that sits like a cap over your shoulder — is the one that is usually hurt. Shoulder injuries occur when someone either attempts to lift too much weight or performs the lift awkwardly and incorrectly. Shoulder strain can best be prevented through a sensible selection of weights and careful lifting technique.

Strained shoulder muscles should be treated with ice packs several times a day for two or three days, and further shoulder exercises should not be undertaken for a week or longer. If the deltoid muscles swell and become very tender, consult a doctor.

When you return to shoulder exercises after a shoulder

strain injury, lift only half (or perhaps even less), of the weight you were attempting when you were injured. Stay with the lighter weights, adding perhaps 5 pounds every second session until you feel confident that your shoulders are strong and free from strain.

Head Injuries

HEAD injuries are not common in weight training. They can, however, occur if the lifter is careless or too ambitious in selecting weights or in assessing his or her own abilities. Head injuries occur when the lifter does not have adequate control of the barbell. This may happen for one of several reasons: the weight is too heavy, he loses his grip, he suffers a blackout from lack of oxygen, or he is off balance. To prevent possible head injuries, be sensible about selecting the weight, use magnesium chalk to ensure a good grip, breathe deeply and continuously, and follow the proper technique for the lift.

If the injury is anything beyond the normal bump or abrasion, see a doctor immediately. Symptoms of a concussion or other possible serious head injury include persistent headache, nausea, vision problems, dizziness, fainting or unconsciousness, mental confusion, and loss of memory. The injured lifter should be taken to a hospital emergency room at once to determine the extent of the injuries and to receive professional medical treatment. Do not return to weight training until given permission by your doctor.

Chest Muscle Strain

MUSCLE strain of the chest can occur if the lifter drops a weight on the chest or pulls one of the pectoral (front) muscles of the chest in attempting to lift a weight that is too heavy. Chest muscle strains heal slowly and cause considerable discomfort. Fortunately, they can be prevented through caution in such lifts as the bench press and by using good sense in the selection of weights for a given stage of development.

Be careful not to reinjure the chest muscles by resuming training too soon. Rest the muscles as much as possible and apply ice packs several times a day or for two or three days or longer. In case of severe pain and swelling in the chest area, see your doctor.

Achilles Tendonitis

THE ACHILLES tendon, a thick tendon at the back of the leg, connects the heel and foot with the back of the calf muscles. Though more commonly injured by runners, the Achilles tendon can be damaged by any exerciser — from weight lifter to football player.

Achilles tendon pull, or Achilles tendonitis as it is more properly called, is a very painful condition. The pain is caused by the inflammation of the sheath within which the tendon slides.

The chance of the ailment occurring can be reduced by developing greater flexibility. Adding a heel lift to your exercise shoes may help, and various yoga exercises can be good preventive medicine. The thigh and lower leg exercises in the CONSUMER GUIDE® program (the Achilles Stretch) are especially recommended for conditioning the leg muscles to prevent Achilles tendonitis.

Achilles tendon pull is ordinarily treated with ice packs until the pain diminishes. When that happens, you can start stretching and limbering exercises. See your doctor, however, if the pain is severe or if swelling occurs.

Hamstring Pull

HAMSTRING pull — the bane of football players, runners, and weight lifters — causes pain in any of the tendons at the back of the lower thighs. Hamstring pull can be prevented by allowing adequate warm-up time before an exercise session and by slowing down or resting when fatigue begins.

Treatment includes the application of ice packs. After the pain has diminished, the muscles can gradually be stretched out. A good stretching exercise consists of raising one leg up to a stool that is 18 to 20 inches high. Keep the knee straight and reach forward to touch the toes. Then alternate legs. If pain persists, see your physician.

Tennis Elbow

TENNIS elbow is a collective term which is used to describe a muscle strain primarily associated with tennis players, but it also afflicts golfers, football players, baseball players and bowlers, jai alai players, and weight lifters. Tennis elbow occurs when rotary movements of the forearms are combined with a firm grip by the hand. Pain and tenderness may extend from the elbow to the hand.

There is no general agreement as to what causes tennis elbow. Nor is there agreement as to how to prevent it. In tennis, the cause is often thought to be too high a service toss or a poor backhand stroke. In weight training, it may result from improper lifting techniques.

If you have suffered from tennis elbow in the past, try the Wrist Curl and the Wrist Extensor exercises in the CONSUMER GUIDE® program to help build the muscular strength needed to prevent a recurrence of the ailment. Regular and vigorous squeezing of a tennis ball or rubber ball can also help (something you can do anywhere, even in a car or at your desk).

Tennis elbow is treated with ice packs. In the more serious versions of the problem, a horizontal sling is prescribed to rest the muscles.

Inflammation Of The Thumb

INFLAMMATION of a tendon of the thumb happens to people who place stress on the thumb through use of dumbbells and barbells, tennis rackets, golf clubs, hammers, etc. A small lump forms under the thumb of the active hand. The lump increases in size, becomes red and very tender, and movement of the thumb joint is limited and painful.

The affected thumb must be kept immobile; massage or movement will make its condition worse. Diathermy (therapeutic heat applications) sometimes relieves the pain, but it is best to have a physician prescribe a course of treatment. You will normally have to cease your weight-training activities until the condition heals.

Sprains

SPRAINS are often confused with strains, but they are quite different. A strain is simply a pulled muscle or tendon. A sprain, on the other hand, results from the stretching or tearing of ligaments which hold bones together at a joint. Any joint can be sprained: finger, wrist, shoulder, knee, ankle, or toe. The most common sprains — those of the ankle and knee — are the ones that will most often force you to curtail your weight-training activities.

Frequently, the average person cannot distinguish between a sprain and a fracture; even a doctor may not be able to tell without X-rays. Sometimes both a sprain and a fracture can result from the same injury. If you are unsure, assume the injury is a fracture and make your next stop a hospital, clinic, or doctor's office.

Symptoms of a sprain include intense pain in the joint (the pain increases when the joint is touched or moved), rapid swelling, and often a black-and-blue discoloration which may not appear until several hours after the sprain.

You can sprain your ankle almost as easily while lifting weights as you can while jumping rope or running. You can also sprain an ankle warming up for your weight-training exercise. Prevention consists of precaution. If you are going to run in place or do side-straddle-hops, be sure there are no obstacles or objects on the floor near you. When lifting, be sure to follow the proper techniques — and be especially careful about balance.

If you do sprain an ankle, you can relieve the pain by resting the joint. To ease the discomfort, elevate the ankle higher than the rest of the body; that will reduce the swelling. As an additional aid, put some support — such as wadded-up clothing or a pillow — under the ankle.

If you suspect that the injury might be a fracture rather than a sprain, do not walk on it until an X-ray confirms that no break in the bone has occurred. If the injury turns out to be no more than a sprain, you can ease the pain by applying a support bandage. Place the middle of an elastic bandage under the foot, in front of the heel; cross ends at the back of the heel and in front, over the instep; loop each end under the rear of the bandage and tie over the instep.

After an ankle sprain, gradually strengthen the foot and leg tissues to help prevent recurrences. Once sprained, an ankle is very susceptible to spraining again. You may have to tape your ankle to give it additional support. Some of the exercises in the CONSUMER GUIDE® program will also be helpful in strengthening the ankle after it heals.

Knee sprains can be serious and extremely painful. If it happens to you, get off the leg immediately and consult a doctor. The doctor will probably recommend ice packs and may even immobilize the leg by splinting it or putting it in a cast.

A sprained knee must be rested until the doctor allows you to renew your weight-training exercises. And then during exercise sessions you must be certain to avoid knee-separation exercises such as full squats, duck walks, and sitting with pressure against fully flexed knees. It is wise, incidentally, to avoid these exercises even if your knees are perfectly healthy.

The heavy-shoe exercises in the CONSUMER GUIDE® program will be helpful in strengthening an injured knee that has mended, Another useful exercise is to sit at the front of a chair, lean backward, and extend the leg fully, tightening the quadriceps (the front or top thigh muscles) so that the kneecap is pulled back. Push on the kneecap with your hand to make sure it is locked in place. Hold this position for forty seconds, feeling the thigh muscles with your fingers to make sure they are contracting strongly. For best results, repeat the exercise about five times.

What causes knee sprains? When the bones mesh properly, the kneecap moves smoothly within a hollow at the lower end of the femur, or thigh bone. When alignment is not correct, the kneecap grinds against one of the slopes in the hollow. Cartilage wears away, and knee sprains result. If you have persistent knee pain or stiffness, consult an orthopedic surgeon for his recommendations.

Knee sprains can be prevented by careful lifting habits and by proper warming up and cooling off. Follow the CONSUMER GUIDE® approach to weight training.

If you sprain a wrist, finger, or toe, treat the injury much as you would a sprained ankle or knee. Rest the injured joint, and then gradually build it back into good shape.

Don't get impatient; if you overwork the injured part, you run a high risk of reinjuring it — perhaps even worse than the original sprain.

Dizziness

DIZZINESS is not a 'hurt' in itself, but it is a very important symptom — a warning signal from your body of an impending and possibly very serious condition. If you become dizzy while lifting (or performing any other exercise), stop exercising immediately. Try to breathe normally but deeply. You may find that you are not only dizzy but also short of breath.

Dizziness may indicate the early stages of heat exhaustion or heat stroke, especially if you are exercising in a hot, humid room, or outdoors on a hot day. It can also occur, however, at normal or below-normal temperatures. Accompanied by shortness of breath or nausea, dizziness may be your body's warning of the presence of circulatory difficulties, the onset of a heart attack, or other major medical problems.

Try to wait out the dizzy spell. When you begin to feel better, start exercising again, slowly and carefully. The dizziness may be just a temporary difficulty that will disappear as quickly as it came. It may also be a symptom of an equilibrium problem. If the dizziness persists, stop exercising and see your doctor.

Your Heart And Exercise

PHYSICAL exercise will not harm a healthy heart. If anything, it will enlarge the heart slightly and make it a more efficient blood-pumping and oxygen-distributing machine.

The key term here is "healthy heart." Since you do not know exactly how healthy your heart is when you begin a physical conditioning program, you should see your physician for a complete physical examination before you embark on any new exercise regimen. A stress electrocardiogram (ECG) should be part of your medical checkup.

Your body itself, though — not somebody else's electronic measurements — should have the final word. It is up to you to listen to your body for any warning signals that your heart may send.

Keep especially alert for extreme or persistent pain down the arms, in the chest, neck, head, ears, or upper abdomen. Another danger sign is if you feel a very heavy pressure on your chest — as though someone were sitting on it. Other symptoms of possible heart problems include extreme tightness, like a clenched fist inside the center of your chest; a feeling somewhat like indigestion; and/or a stuffiness high in your stomach or low in your throat. If your symptoms of pain or discomfort resemble any of these, stop exercising and call your doctor.

The CONSUMER GUIDE® program is not designed as a builder or strengthener of your heart. For that you will need a cardiovascular exercise program, like the CONSUMER GUIDE® running program. In fact, anyone who plans to embark upon a body-building program would be wise to get his or her cardiovascular system in shape before concentrating on improvements in appearance, strength, and muscular endurance.

A Final Note

MOST OF the hurts associated with exercising are preventable. And, of course, it is far more sensible to prevent them than to treat them after they have occurred. Injuries are usually the result of carelessness, fatigue, or overexertion. When an injury disables a muscle or a group of muscles, postpone full exercise of that body part until the muscles heal.

The CONSUMER GUIDE® program is itself good protection against many injuries that are common in daily life. Toning your body and strengthening your muscles will help you avoid many of the aches and pains that afflict your more sedentary friends and associates.

Manufacturers ballyhoo hundreds of body-building gadgets and machines, claiming miraculous results with minimal effort. But CONSUMER GUIDE® recommends that the beginner invest in nothing more exotic than a basic set of weights.

The CONSUMER GUIDE® Name~Brand Product Evaluation

TO EMBARK upon the CONSUMER GUIDE® program for building a better body, all you really need is a basic set of weights (barbells or dumbbells). You can get by without weighted boots if you have a pair of very heavy workshoes or outdoor boots. You can also forego the specially designed weight-training bench. An ordinary bench of the proper proportions will be adequate. Similarly, you can use a remnant of a shag rug or indoor-outdoor carpeting instead of a mat.

If you do substitute, though, make certain that what you use is safe. A bench must be sturdy and strong enough to support you and the weights; a rug should offer good traction. Once you are firmly committed to a weight-training routine, moreover, you really should invest in quality equipment. The cost is not great (at least for basic gear), and the benefits justify the expenditure.

First, let's look at the basic equipment you will need for the CONSUMER GUIDE® body-building program. Afterwards, we will discuss some of the other pieces of equipment (ranging from a relatively useless $5 arm-pull exerciser to an $11,000 mini-gym) available for body building or body toning.

Barbells And Dumbbells

A BARBELL set (bar and weight plates) constitutes the basic equipment in the CONSUMER GUIDE® program. Available from firms that specialize in weight-training gear (York or Weider, for example), barbells can also be obtained (usually much less expensively) from department, chain, discount, and sporting goods stores.

The bar itself should be at least four, but no longer than about six, feet long. About an inch in diameter, it should have a sleeve that fits and revolves around it, an inside collar to separate the weights from the sleeve, and an outside collar to hold the weights in place. With some sets, the collars must be locked in place with a wrench. With sleeve and collars, a bar will usually weigh 10 or 25 pounds.

Weight plates are available in either uncoated cast iron or vinyl-covered sand or concrete. Cast-iron weights are stronger and more expensive, while the vinyl-covered ones are quieter but a bit more fragile. If you are lifting on the second floor or on a hardwood floor, opt for the vinyl-coated ones since they present less of an annoyance to the people beneath you and do less damage to the floor. In the event that you're lifting on a concrete garage floor or basement, then the cast-iron weights are the way to go.

A beginner's barbell set (generally 110 pounds) includes an assortment of weight plates totaling 90 pounds in 2½-,

Curling Bar from Bell Foundry

5-, 10-, and 25-pound sizes. Although somewhat rare, it is possible to get 1-and 1¼-pound plates, and you should get some if you can. The light weights give you more flexibility when progressing with your lifting program. Sometimes a five-pound jump is too much, making a 2- or 2½-pound jump more suitable.

The bar itself should come with a sleeve. The sleeve permits easier lifting and rotation of the bar as you move it through the exercise. A bar with a sleeve may be more expensive, but the extra expense is well worth it.

Four metal collars (two inside and two on the outside) usually encircle each bar and are used to hold the plates in place. Both types of collars contain set screws for creating a secure fit on the bar. Some of the collars require a special wrench, while others have a built-in wrench for loosening and tightening the set screw. The outside collars with the built-in wrench are preferable because they make changing weight levels easier. Most manufacturers offer both types, generally charging a few dollars extra for the collars with the built-in wrench.

The best barbell sets cost from $150 to $200. Inexpensive — though adequate sets for beginners — can be found in the $20 to $30 price range. If you order a set, though, don't forget shipping charges — they can add another $15 or $20 to your purchase price. Below are some of the companies which manufacture or distribute basic barbell sets.

Bell Foundry Company
5310 Southern Avenue
South Gate, California 90280

Montgomery Ward & Co., Inc.
535 W. Chicago Avenue
Chicago, Illinois 60607

Sears Roebuck And Co.
Sears Tower
Chicago, Illinois 60684

Weider Health And Fitness, Inc.
21100 Erwin Street
Woodland Hills, California 91364

York Barbell Company, Inc.
P.O. Box 1707
York, Pennsylvania 17405

The dumbbell can best be described as a short barbell, 8 to 18 inches in length. Many dumbbells are cast in one piece and therefore are of fixed poundage. Fixed-weight dumbbells are available in poundages ranging from 3 to over 75 pounds, but most range between 3 and 40 pounds.

The biggest problem with the fixed-weight dumbbell is that you have to buy a host of them in order to progress with your program properly. As a result, CONSUMER GUIDE® suggests that you try to purchase a dumbbell set (two of them) with a bar 14 to 18 inches long and one inch in diameter that comes with interchangeable weights, sleeves, and collars.

Like barbells, dumbbells come in cast-iron and vinyl-coated versions. If you lift on a concrete floor, the metal

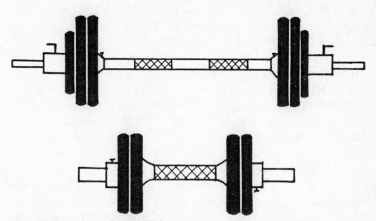

Barbell (top) has outside collars with built-in wrenches. Dumbbell (bottom) has outside collars with set screws that must be tightened with a separate wrench. Collars with the built-in wrench are preferable.

ones are best because they are more durable. If you're lifting in a house or on the second floor, though, then get the vinyl-covered plates. In either case, buy collars with the built-in wrench.

Other Basic Equipment

IRON BOOTS, attached to the feet with straps, have center holes through which short metal bars are inserted and to which plates are attached in order to bring the weight of the boots up to the desired poundage. Generally used for exercises designed to strengthen the muscles controlling leg movements at the knees or the hips, these metal boots are actually little more than shoes with a plate strapped on.

Again, like barbells and dumbbells, iron boots offer a choice between vinyl and metal plates. The collars are extremely important for easy taking off and putting on, but sleeves are not necessary since the bar is inserted into the loop on the boot itself.

Good lifting benches consist of either wood or metal framing and padding. They are usually 10 to 14 inches wide, about 18 inches high and from three to five feet in length. The best benches have a metal holder to support the barbell before and after bench pressing. Many of the good benches are adjustable in the back and leg areas for added versatility. Ranging from about $15 or $20 for the simplest to $150 for a deluxe unit, lifting benches are available from sporting goods stores, mail order and catalog retailers, and department stores.

Many of the chest as well as abdominal exercises are performed from a bench or incline bench. The bench is useful for chest exercises because it allows the shoulders and arms to hang below the level of the chest, thus permitting the pectoralis major muscles of the upper chest to be worked from a lengthened position. But before rushing out to buy a bench, think of some alternatives. You can improvise at home by placing a board between two chairs; just make sure that the board will support you while you exercise and that there's enough room for you to lie straddling the board while your arms hang below shoulder level.

Incline trunk curls are only possible on a strong bench, but again there is no need to buy one. You can make one easily that will satisfy most requirements.

Supplementary Body-Building Devices

OF THE MANY body-building devices available for purchase today, none can do any more for you than a simple set of barbells and dumbbells. Even the multi-station weight-training machines that cost thousands of dollars will not enable you to accomplish anything more (or any faster or easier) than you could with a basic set of weights and a well-conceived program of exercise. Some of the items, in fact, are virtually worthless, and body builders should be wary of spending money on gear that will not produce results or will produce results equivalent to those obtainable with a less-expensive set of weights.

Without a doubt, the most common of these other devices are those designed for pulling and stretching. Ranging in complexity from simple elastic ropes that can be hooked over a doorknob to sophisticated spring-powered gadgets that cost considerably more but do exactly the same thing, pulling and stretching devices can function in a variety of ways.

Rubber Stretchers

RUBBER STRETCHERS are highly elastic pieces of rubber with loops at the ends for easier gripping and holding. You grip the loops and then pull your hands apart as far as possible. Or you can place a foot in one loop and pull with the one arm.

While the rubber stretcher can develop strength for specific areas and specific muscles, it is of questionable value because it doesn't allow for any adjustments to accommodate changes in strength. A very weak person is often unable to move a rubber stretcher while a strong person will find the resistance too low. Therefore, rubber stretchers cannot be recommended.

Chest Pulls

CHEST PULLS operate on the same principles as the rubber stretchers; the object is to pull the handles apart, and how far you can pull them depends upon your strength. Usually made up of two detachable handles with one to five rubber or steel springs in between, they are better than the rubber stretchers in that they allow you to make adjustments according to strength.

The chest pull can help develop muscle strength in specific muscles — particularly the arms, shoulders, and chest. But it should not be used by any person with a cardiac condition. As with the rubber stretcher, it is very difficult to know how much work is being done, and — despite the fact that springs can be added or removed — little leeway is made for changes in strength. Another drawback is that when the springs are stretched they can trap the user's skin and cause a nasty pinch when released. Like rubber stretchers, chest pulls are not recommended.

The highly-advertised Bullworker is basically a resistance device. Consisting of a rather remarkable 34-inch cylinder with another cylinder set on springs inside, the Bullworker has pulling cords at the sides. One can perform resistance exercises (24 of which are described in the handbook that comes with the device) by pushing the two cylinders together against the tension of the springs. While it is one of the more effective pieces of resistance equipment, the Bullworker still offers nothing one cannot achieve with a set of weights. Since it only weighs about five pounds,though, it is highly portable — you can take it along on trips.

Exer-Genie, Apollo Exerciser, And Exer-Gym

SIMILAR TYPES of products, the Exer-Genie, Apollo Exerciser (from the Physical Fitness Institute of America), and Exer-Gym can be used to help improve muscle strength, muscle endurance, and body appearance. They usually come with — in addition to the exercise device itself — an instructional booklet, carrying case, the handles, foot board, and assorted materials. Optional materials that can be purchased include a cassette, workout charts, and additional nylon cord and straps.

The design is similar for all three exercise products. The top of the shaft (enclosed in a casing) is a metal loop or eye. A nylon line leads out of the shaft through the loop, and a handle is attached to each of the two ends of the line. Resistance, preset by revolving the casing around the shaft, is achieved by friction as the specially braided line winds around the shaft. The amount of line passing over the shaft determines the approximate resistance in pounds pulled. The amount of resistance can be varied for individual exercises.

The Exer-Genie program can be cited as typical. A six-minute program for general conditioning, it combines a series of exercises called the "Big Four" with two additional exercises — the bicycle and row. The program, to be done daily, recommends that the "Big Four" be repeated four times, pausing a minute or two between repetitions until breathing is normal and the pulse drops to 120.

The "Big Four" exercises begin with a 10-minute isometric hold obtained by applying finger pressure on a nylon cord looped over the handle of the exercise device. The preset resistance is constant as long as no other pressure is placed against the rope. But when strong pressure is applied against it — e.g., a finger pressed against the handle — the rope becomes impossible to move, regardless of the preset resistance. Following the isometric hold, finger pressure is released gradually, and the following exercises are performed in sequence: the dead lift, leg press, biceps curl, upright curl, and the standing press.

Following the "Big Four," the individual exercises for one more minute to complete the six-minute program. He or she can do either the bicycling or rowing exercise, alternating daily. The bicycling exercise is for the legs and derriere, while the rowing exercise is for the shoulders, upper back, and abdominal muscles.

Among the attractive features of the Exer-Genie and similar products are the following:

1. Muscle groups can be initially isolated and worked by a variety of special exercises.
2. Exercises can be adapted from highly sophisticated weight-training equipment and simulated with the device.
3. Various sports techniques can be combined with body conditioning training, since the various movements can be simulated and performed under controlled resistance.
4. The equipment is less expensive than weight-training equipment, much easier to store and carry, and can be set up and used anywhere.
5. The time needed for a complete exercise routine comparable to weight training is generally less.
6. The devices combine the advantages of isometric contractions for maximum strength development with the range of motion that weight training provides, while providing the added benefit of maintaining a steady resistance throughout the entire range of movement.

One of the biggest criticisms of these products concerns

the difficulty in knowing exactly how much tension is programmed into the product. As a consequence, people who use them are faced with the problem of recording accurately where they are and what kind of improvement they have achieved.

CONSUMER GUIDE® recommends that the Exer-Genie, Apollo Exerciser, or Exer-Gym be used only as an adjunct to your personalized weight-training program. They do not, as claimed, constitute a complete physical fitness program. Used conscientiously, they will build strength, improve appearance, and help tone muscles, but CONSUMER GUIDE® still advocates standard weight-training equipment for building a better body.

Body Trimmers

BODY TRIMMERS, the rage during 1975 and 1976, are simply rope systems which you attach to a wall, door, etc. You lie flat on the floor with your feet and hands attached to the ropes. As you move your leg downward your arm will be pulled forward and vice versa. Thus, body trimmers use one set of muscles to work against another set. If an individual can regulate the resistance he or she might derive some benefit, but in most cases calisthenics can produce better results at far less cost.

The jump rope is a very useful exercise device, and it is also one of the least expensive. You can make your own jump rope with 9 to 10 feet of window sash cord or braided cotton clothesline; just wrap the surplus around your hands when you jump. A regular jump rope is much more satisfactory, however. You can buy cheap ones from sporting goods houses or mail-order catalogs for $3 and up, but the rope from AMF Whitely (at about $11) is an exceptionally good one. The rope is leather and the wooden handles move on concealed ball bearings.

Other Body-Building Gadgets

A GADGET called Sit-a-Shape can be attached to the bottom of most doors. Useful for warming-up and cooling-down exercises, it will hold your feet in position for sit-ups.

Available from Sears, Sit-a-Shape retails for about $10.

The Lift-Up Machine from Wolverine Sports has weights on the end of a rod which you squat to lift. Standard weights can be attached to the end of the rod to vary the weight load. Designed to strengthen and tone the muscles of the arms, shoulders, abdomen, and legs, the unit is equipped with rubber pads to prevent marring. The price is about $39.

The Abdominal Board, also from Wolverine Sports, strengthens the abdominal and leg muscles by permitting you to do sit-ups while your feet are elevated one, two, or three feet higher than your head. The foam-padded plywood board measures 84 inches long and 18 inches wide, and it has a strap to hold your feet down. The feet of the board are rubber-padded to protect floors. The Abdominal Board sells for about $45.

Rowing machines — once found only in gymnasiums and YMCA's — are now gaining popularity for home use. Consisting essentially of a seat that moves along a steel frame in response to the user's rowing motion, the rowing machine can provide a good workout for muscles. In fact the exercise can be so strenuous that it should be avoided by anyone with heart problems or high blood pressure.

Several kinds of rowing machines are available. Most of them are quite compact and will fit into or nearby any exercise room. They will not replace weights, however, and they are considerably more expensive — ranging from about $160 to more than $1000.

Lat Machines

IT IS DIFFICULT to exercise the latissimus dorsi muscles from the standing position. These are the muscles on your back that pull your arms downward to the sides of your body. The lat muscles are used in the chinning of a bar and in swimming the breaststroke. A lat machine provides resistance via pulleys or handles when a person pulls down to lift the weight on the end of a wire. In so doing it helps in the development of a broad upper back.

Only advanced weight trainers should consider the lat

Lift-Up Machine from Wolverine Sports

machine essential. It is hardly worth the expense for the beginner.

Leg Pressing Machines

MANY WELL-EQUIPPED gymnasiums have leg pressing machines. With this piece of equipment, the lifter lies on his back, presses his legs against a loaded platform, and extends his legs forward.

For most purposes, the exercises outlined in this book are adequate for developing the leg muscles, and no beginner in body building need spend as much as a leg pressing machine costs. Of course, weight-training enthusiasts are as fond of the leg press machine as they are of the lat machine.

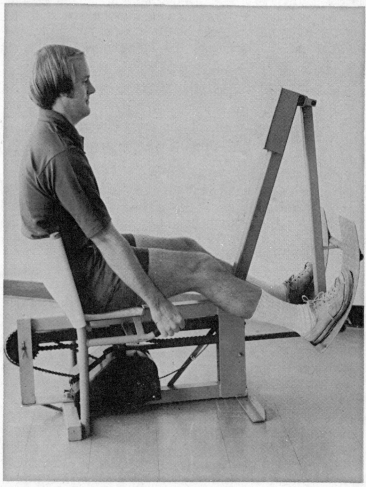

Sitting Leg Press from Mini-Gym

Standards

METAL STANDARDS — used to support the barbells at a designated height from the floor — are convenient when performing certain exercises, but they are not necessary for the beginner.

Head Strap

THE HEAD STRAP is a device made of canvas webbing which is worn like a cap around the top of the head. Plates can be attached to a chain on the head strap for development of neck muscles. No beginner in weight training needs a head strap.

Home Gymnasium Equipment

IF YOU have the room and the budget, you can acquire any of several very expensive "mini-gyms" for your bodybuilding activities.

One of the most versatile of these machines is the Folding Gym. Requiring only a 3 x 8 foot wall or floor space in your exercise area, it can provide six different activities. The Folding Gym offers an 8-foot horizontal ladder 36 inches wide and 7 to 8 feet high, heavy rings, a climbing rope, and an adjustable chinning bar. Made by Todd-Phelps Company, the Folding Gym retails for about $300.

A more versatile gym machine is the 16-Station Weight Machine from Program Aids, Inc. The 16 stations include leg press endurance, power position and support seat, chest and shoulder press, high lat (back and chest) pulldown, quad (thigh and pelvis muscles) low pulley, calf flexor and toe raise, chinning and dipping stations, hip flexor, abdominal board, squat station, rowing, leg extension and curl, back hyperextension, neck and wrist conditioners, and many other features. The price for this machine, installed in your home, runs about $4500, plus delivery charges. Program Aids also makes a Nine-Station Weight Machine, a unit that sells for $3400 plus delivery charges. It offers a two-position leg press, chest press, shoulder press, high lat pull, quad pulley, dip bar, nine level

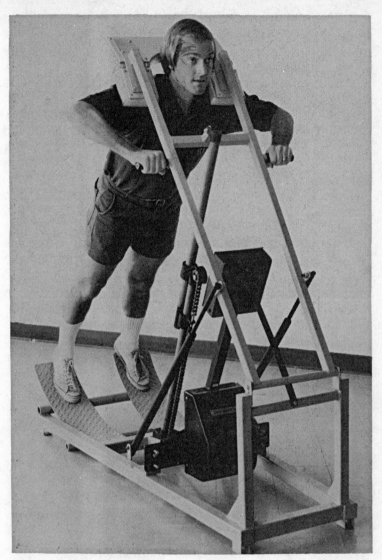

Squat Thrust from Mini-Gym

abdominal board, chinning station, and rowing.

The Muscle Builder from Todd-Phelps Company provides weights set on vertical poles. The weights slide up and down smoothly without lubrication, and each weight has noise-free rubber bumpers. A prone bench is part of the unit. A 120-pound unit (which must be screwed to the wall), it costs about $500.

The Latissimus Body Builder attaches to a wall and is designed to help develop the shoulders, chest, back, arms, and waist while improving coordination and endurance. Pulling down on the bar lifts up weights. The 285-pound model costs $350 and the 385-pound model costs $420. Extra five-pound weights are $5.40 each. The unit is another product of Todd-Phelps Company.

Duplex Pulley Weights from Porter Equipment attach to the wall and help to develop shoulders, arms, chest, and back. They are somewhat like the Latissimus Body Builder in that pulling on the pulleys raises 5- to 17-pound weights on each side. More weights can be added. The machine costs $245, plus shipping, and cartage costs are added according to weight.

Mini-Gym, Inc. offers a number of gym machines. The Squat Thrust (about $600 plus shipping cost) is designed to develop maximum power in the legs and back. The Sit-

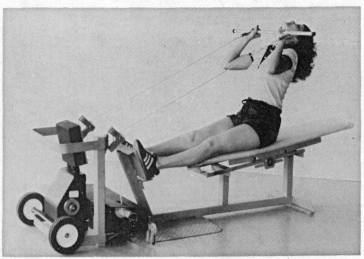

All-Purpose Unit from Mini-Gym

Fourteen-Station Trainer-Matic from GSC Athletic

ting Leg Press (about $550 plus freight charges) offers a number of leg muscle exercises. The All-Purpose Unit (about $600 plus freight charges) is an overall exerciser which helps build leg and lower back strength. Isokinetic resistance adjusts to each individual's efforts.

The Fixed Lat Machine from Wolverine Sports attaches to a wall and is designed to develop the back and upper arms. You can exercise while standing, kneeling, or squatting, facing front or rear. It costs about $60.

The Fourteen-Station Trainer-Matic from GSC Athletic, includes a 200-pound pulley, a 200-pound latissimus pulldown, a six-way adjustable arm exerciser, 20 major barbell exercisers (225 pounds), a quad pulley that handles two people at once, combination hip flexing and chin stations, wrist and forearm workouts, leg flexing and extension, abdominal board, back hyperextension, neck developer, a dipping bar, and a grip developer. All weights have automatic self-locking safety keys. The price is about $3950 delivered. GSC Athletic's Six-Station Trainer-Matic includes a 150-pound low pulley, a 200-pound overhead pulldown, a 260-pound six-way adjustable lifting arm, a 260-pound barbell exerciser, a 410-pound seated leg press, a leg flexer and extension. It provides workouts on all major muscle groups. The price is about $3100, delivered.

The Pro 16 Professional Gym from Professional Gym, Inc. is probably the ultimate in gym machines. Don't even consider it unless you have an area measuring about 20 x 20 feet to accommodate it. The unit stands about 84 inches high and has 16 stations: a leg press endurance position, a high support seat power position, a chest press, a shoulder press, a high lat pulldown, a quad low pulley, a calf flexor and toe raise, a chinning station, a dipping station, a hip flexor, an abdominal board, a squat station, rowing, leg extension and leg curl, back hyperextension, neck conditioner, and a wrist conditioner. All heavy press stations connect directly to the weight stacks (no cables), and locking weight selector keys are provided for safety. The price is approximately $5000 plus shipping charges (shipping weight is 4,300 pounds).

You can order perhaps the most elaborate home gymnasium from Program Aids, Inc. A luxurious chrome-plated five-station machine with heavy vinyl padding, it sells for about $11,000.

Mail-Order Suppliers

THE FOLLOWING athletic equipment companies will send you additional information and catalogs on the bodybuilding gear they market by mail-order.

Cran Barry, Inc.
2 Lincoln Avenue
Marblehead, MA. 01945

Exer-Genie, Inc.
P.O. Box 3320
Fullerton, CA. 92634

Exer-Gym
P.O. Box 100
Opelika, AL 36801

Flaghouse, Inc.
18 West 18th Street
New York City, NY. 10011

Gopher Athletic Supply Co.
2125 NW 4th Street
Box 0, Owatonna, MN. 55060

GSC Athletic Equipment
600 North Pacific Avenue
P.O. Box 1710, San Pedro, CA. 90733

Jayfro Corp.
P.O. Box 400
Waterford, CT. 06385

Mini-Gym, Inc.
Box 266
Independence, MO. 64051

Passon's, Inc.
1017 Arch Street
Philadelphia, PA. 19107

Physical Fitness Institute of America
851 Lake Shore Blvd.
Incline Village, NV. 89450

Porter Equipment Co.
9555 Irving Park Rd.
Schiller Park, IL. 60176

Professional Gym, Inc.
805 Cherokee
Marshall, MO 65340

Program Aids, Inc.
161 MacQuesten Parkway
Mount Vernon, NY. 10550

Todd-Phelps
1945 Palmer Avenue
Larchmont, NY. 10538

U. S. Games, Inc.
Box EG 874
Melbourne, FL. 32935
(800-327-0484, Bill Gleason)

Wolverine Sports
745 State Circle
Ann Arbor, MI. 48104

**Your home is the best place
to put the CONSUMER
GUIDE® program into action.
If you decide to join a
commercial gymnasium, be
sure to investigate before
you invest.**

Gyms, Health Clubs, And Other Facilities

IF YOU cannot work out at home, or if you prefer working out in the company of others, you can choose from a host of facilities that will suit your purposes. There are virtually thousands of commercial gymnasiums and health clubs, some offering their facilities on a fee or rental basis, with others involving contractual arrangements.

Some gyms and clubs offer organized programs of exercise, ranging from simple calisthenics classes to professional tutoring in weight training. Many have excellent facilities, including quality weight-training equipment. Others, though, offer only worthless apparatus: e.g., vibrating belts and other types of machines designed to work on you rather than have you work on yourself. Building a better body requires exertion, and any gear that promises results without effort is fraudulent; facilities promoting such gear are to be avoided.

There is nothing new about public gymnasiums, health spas, and fitness clubs. The ancient Greeks used them as did the Romans. Health resorts and spas flourished throughout Europe — especially Germany, Switzerland, and Scandinavia — and still do today.

Various Indian tribes of North and South America took vapor baths and exercised in hot springs. Colonists established a spa at Stafford Springs, Connecticut, in the late 1600s; it flourished until the early 1800s. George Washington, Alexander Hamilton, and Thomas Jefferson frequented the spas of Virginia.

Gymnasium Facilities

TODAY, ONE need not seek out hot spring spas in order to enjoy public health facilities. Such facilities are frequently within walking distance of your home. Junior high schools, high schools, community colleges, and universities often offer use of their gymnasiums to the public during non-school hours.

Of all the organizations offering public gymnasium facilities, though, the Young Men's Christian Association (YMCA) is undoubtedly the best known. Look for the Young Men's Christian Association in your phone book. If you don't find it, you can write to the Young Men's Christian Association, 291 Broadway, New York, NY 10007, for the phone number of the YMCA nearest you. YMCA facilities are usually open to both men and women, but if you want to get in touch with an all-women's organization, write to the Young Women's Christian Association (YWCA), 600 Lexington Avenue, New York, NY 10022.

The Jewish Community Centers, serving both men and women, likewise offer excellent facilities. You can get information about the gyms of these centers from the National Jewish Welfare Board, 15 East 26th Street, New York, NY 10010. More than 300 such gyms exist, and you don't have to be Jewish to enroll. The Christian Youth Organization (CYO) also has gym facilities in many large cities.

In addition, of course, are the commercial gyms. Some are bright and clean with first-rate equipment; others are dingy and dirty with little or no quality body-building gear. Still others feature abundant chrome-plated equipment in a luxurious setting, but all too often the equipment is designed more for appearance than function.

The only way you can find out which facilities are best for you is by visiting various gyms and observing firsthand. To shop around, look under "Gymnasiums" in the yellow pages of your telephone book. Call and ask what facilities or programs each gym offers; then go visit the places. It is very important that you go to the gym in person; descriptions given over the phone or in a color brochure cannot be relied upon for total accuracy when selecting a facility.

When choosing gym facilities, use the following list of questions to help you determine whether any given place is the right one for you.

1. What kinds of equipment does the facility have?
2. What will be the daily, weekly, or monthly cost based on the number of times the user will actually work out in the gym?
3. Must users sign a contract? If so, what kind of a contract? For how long? Can the contract be canceled and the money refunded after three days of using the facilities? (More and more states are requiring such a "cooling-off" period.) Also, can the contract be canceled and some of the money returned if the user becomes ill, seriously injured, or dies? Are all the provisions of the contract clear?
4. Does the gym carry liability insurance?
5. Can the gym guarantee use of the facilities at hours appropriate to the user? Don't accept verbal assurance, go to the gym at your preferred exercise hour and see whether you will have to wait in line in order to utilize the exercise equipment.
6. Does the gym have any auxiliary features such as a tennis court, a handball court, or a running track? How busy are they at your preferred exercise time?
7. Are there separate facilities for women? If men and women use the same equipment, do men get the preferred hours?
8. Is the gym a place where you would like to spend three to four hours a week? Are the people friendly? Do you feel comfortable there? Is it clean and well-maintained? Does it have adequate locker room and shower facilities?
9. Are the trainers and attendants competent? Do they have academic credentials or several years of

training in the physical fitness or weight-training fields? Talk with some of them in order to make an assessment.
10. Does the health club or gym provide classes geared to your needs, that is, classes for beginners, intermediates and advanced participants?

Health And Fitness Clubs

HEALTH clubs cater to an estimated three million Americans — and the businesses gross nearly one billion dollars a year. Some of these health clubs are small with limited facilities; others are elaborate and contain the most up-to-date and expensive equipment.

Among the most well-known health clubs in the United States are those listed under the following names or franchises: Vic Tanny, Jack LaLanne, Holiday Health Spas, Nautilus Fitness Centers, Elaine Powers, Silhouette/ American, and European Health Spas.

People join those health clubs (or similar ones that are locally rather than nationally based) for a variety of reasons: the idea of group exercise, the plush environment, the social contacts — the list is endless.

Whatever the reason you seek to join a health club, you should be aware of certain considerations before taking out a membership. Here are some guidelines to follow when evaluating a health club:

1. Tour the facilities.
2. Read the contract carefully. Take it home with you to study. If the club won't let you do this, the contract is not likely to be a good one.
3. Be sure the contract commits you to no more than two years. One year is better.
4. Be certain the contract provides for a three day "cooling off" period before the contract legally takes effect. It should also specify a "use-of-facility" arrangement so that you can use the club during those three days when making your own judgment.
5. Before signing any contract, talk to people who currently belong or have belonged to the club.

6. Check with the Better Business Bureau or local chamber of commerce regarding any complaints against the club.

Keep in mind that anyone can open a health club. In most states, no licensing or test of competence is required. And in many instances, you will be faced with a "hard-sell" approach.

In an effort to diminish high-pressure tactics, the Federal Trade Commission has proposed regulations to correct any deceptive and misleading advertising or sales presentations used by many health clubs. Part of this FTC effort is the advocacy of the three-day trial period in every contract. This would give a consumer time to visit and use the health club on a trial basis, and to reconsider the apparent benefits and costs. If the customer cancels the contract within the stated cooling-off period, all fees must be returned.

The Federal Trade Commission has issued a list of unfair practices uncovered in its investigation of health clubs. You may want to use the list when assessing the specific health club you are considering.

1. Using high-pressure selling tactics.
2. Closing facilities or going out of business without making arrangements to meet contractual obligations to customers.
3. Selling membership contracts to customers who are not physically qualified to take part in the activities of the club.
4. Offering bargains that do not exist.
5. Misrepresenting the facilities available and the qualifications of the employees.
6. Making false claims about the effectiveness of weight reduction and figure shaping programs.
7. Having unfair cancellation and refund policies.

Many health clubs belong to the Association of Physical Fitness Centers, a trade association dedicated to upgrading the industry. Dr. Jimmy Johnson, executive director of the association, points out that member clubs are being encouraged to emphasize cardiovascular fitness as well as muscle toning, strength, and endurance facilities.

CONSUMER GUIDE® recommends that, if at all possible, you conduct your weight-training activities at home. At commercial facilities (including both the bad and good ones) you will be working out with people who are much more proficient than you, possibly making adherence to your personalized CONSUMER GUIDE® program a source of self-consciousness. If you must go outside, however, be sure that the facilities are worth what you pay and that you do not get locked into a contract with which you will be unhappy.

Appendix:
What Is
Physical Fitness?

RIGHT AT the start let's understand one thing: There is a good bit of confusion over the term "physical fitness."

To each of us physical fitness may mean something different. For some it is the ability to do thirty push-ups; or it may be the ability to run a mile and a half nonstop or to get through the day without fatigue. Or it may simply mean looking or feeling good. Physicians generally regard fitness as freedom from disease; physiologists examine responses to certain stimuli; and physical educators look for the capacity of human performance. All of these have a place in a full definition of fitness.

In our definition, fitness encompasses the basic physical well-being necessary for a full and healthy life. The President's Council on Physical Fitness and Sports has issued a concise statement that sums up pretty nicely what physical fitness is all about: "The ability to carry out daily tasks with vigor and alertness, without undue fatigue, and with ample energy to enjoy leisure-time pursuits and to meet unforeseen emergencies."[1]

The Foundations Of Fitness

PHYSICAL fitness is dependent upon two basic components, which we shall refer to as "organic" and "dynamic" fitness. Both are necessary ingredients in overall physical fitness, and it is the interaction between the two that determines how fit we are.

By "organic fitness" we mean the characteristics of the particular flesh-and-blood body we each possess, inherited from our parents and affected by aging and perhaps by illness or accident. Here we are speaking of body size, build, and other physical features. This is what we're talking about when we say a person comes from "strong stock" or when we speak of another individual as having certain physical limitations or difficulties. This "organism" is essentially static, and difficult or even impossible to alter. Your organic fitness level determines your potential for overall physical fitness.

"Dynamic fitness" is much more variable. This term is used here to refer to the readiness and capacity of the body for action and movement. It has to do not with the ultimate potential for (or we could say limitations on) action, but with the degree to which this potential is realized.

Imagine a "fitness continuum" with two extremes: the ideal "fit" American on one end and the completely incapacitated (and even degenerating) individual on the other. Obviously, people with heart lesions, metabolic diseases, neurological dysfunction, and other disabilities are not in good health, nor are they fit. At the same time, people who are basically in good health yet are very inactive would also be low on the fitness continuum because they are deficient in dynamic fitness, lacking such characteristics as strength and endurance. Dr. George Sheehan, M.D., says that most Americans are in this latter condition, and he calls it "good health; lousy shape."[2]

Organic and dynamic fitness must both be considered in any evaluation of fitness; neither predominates. For example, you may have inherited a body that could conceivably run a four-minute mile, but smoking, inactivity, stress, and poor diet may result in your being able to walk only a mile in twenty minutes. In other words, your life style has hampered the development of the important components of fitness — circulo-respiratory endurance. Although you are organically sound, your dynamic fitness is low and your overall fitness suffers greatly.

This works the other way, too. You may have inherited a capacity to run only a six-minute mile, yet daily jogging, no smoking, and good diet permit you to work close to your potential. In that case, your overall fitness would be considered quite good.

On the whole, organic fitness is difficult to alter and represents a "given factor" in our chances for all-around physical fitness. We can't change our height, leg and arm length, or general build. If we have inherited physical handicaps of any kind or have experienced an illness or accident that has left a physical disability, we must operate within certain limits that others may not have to cope with.

Dynamic fitness, on the other hand, can be improved greatly merely by doing something about it. Whatever your stature and biological characteristics, you can advance dramatically on the fitness continuum by getting enough of the right kind of exercise.

Components Of Dynamic Fitness

MOST THEORISTS agree that dynamic fitness consists of five major components: muscular strength, muscular endurance, flexibility, circulo-respiratory endurance, and good body composition.[3] These can all be significantly improved through proper exercise. Which components are developed depends upon the type of exercise selected.

Muscular Strength

MUSCULAR strength is measured by the amount of force that can be exerted by a single contraction of a muscle. A reasonable degree of muscle strength is important for many reasons. It's necessary for such household tasks as carrying out the garbage, lifting groceries, and moving furniture, as well as for coping with emergency situations. Adequate shoulder and back strength is needed to help avoid slouching and to maintain proper support for the back. Strength is also necessary in order to have good skill performance in many types of athletics. Muscular strength is developed with exercise such as weight training, isometrics, isokinetics, or selected calisthenics.

Muscular Endurance

MUSCULAR endurance is measured by the length of time a type of activity can be sustained by particular muscles — that is, how many times a person can repeat an exercise, such as arm circles, push-ups, and sit-ups.

We need muscle endurance to continue in any given activity over a period of time. For example, strength is needed to assume a correct postural position, but muscle endurance is essential in order to maintain that posture throughout the day.

Many jobs require muscle endurance. A typist needs sufficient forearm, shoulder, and back muscle endurance to type all day. A bricklayer needs a high degree of muscle endurance to work continuously. Muscle endurance is needed in order to stand or sit at any job for several hours a day without becoming overly fatigued. Without muscle endurance, a person tires quickly and his or her efficiency suffers, thereby cutting down on productivity.

Muscle endurance is improved through calisthenics, weight training, and aerobic exercises.

Flexibility

FLEXIBILITY is the range of motion possible at the joints. For example, from a sitting position — legs straight out in front — can you touch your toes without bending your knees? If you can't, the muscles, tendons, and ligaments of the lower back and back of the legs are not sufficiently flexible.

Flexibility is necessary in all the major joints of the body to help avoid muscle pulls and strains. Improved flexibility will result in fewer injuries, better performance, and more freedom of movement. Lack of flexibility can contribute to lower back pain and those maddening muscle and joint injuries that occur in adults when they attempt to reach for an object underneath a desk or on top of a shelf.

To improve overall flexibility, you must work separately on each joint or group of joints in the body. Flexibility is improved through slow, stretching exercises, continually repeated over a period of time.

Circulo-Respiratory Endurance

CIRCULO-RESPIRATORY endurance consists of the ability of the heart, blood, and blood vessels to transport oxygen to the muscle cells, process the oxygen in those cells, and carry off the resultant waste products. Sometimes this is called "aerobic fitness," "aerobic power," or "cardiovascular fitness."

Many physiologists feel that this is the most important component of physical fitness. It determines how well you can persist in large muscle activities for a sustained period of time. A high level of circulo-respiratory endurance is needed for many daily tasks and to handle the unexpected without placing dangerous stress on the body.

Moreover, there is considerable evidence that activities or exercises that improve circulo-respiratory endurance may help reduce certain cardiovascular disease risk factors in adults. That is, they may provide what is called "cardio-protective resistance" (help prevent heart attacks, in layman's terms).

With a high degree of circulo-respiratory endurance, fatigue is postponed and work can be carried on for longer periods. Circulo-respiratory endurance is important when participating in most sports.

The best exercises for improving circulo-respiratory endurance or cardiovascular endurance are walking, jogging, swimming, dancing, bicycling, and any activities that are of a continuous, dynamic nature involving large muscle groups of the body.

No one can say yet that these exercises will help you live longer, but we do know that they improve heart health and lessen fatigue, so that you will be more productive while you are alive.

CONSUMER GUIDE® is among those who believe that circulo-respiratory endurance is the most important component of dynamic fitness. This type of exercise will slow down fatigue, increase energy, reduce body weight, and reduce several coronary heart disease risk factors. No other component of fitness can make all those claims.

Body Composition

RESEARCH has shown that many degenerative diseases, including heart disease, diabetes, and arthritis, are related to obesity. It is important to note that the reference is to obesity and not to overweight; they are not synonymous. The distinction is simple: "Properly speaking, an obese person is one who carries around an excessive amount of body fat. An overweight person, on the other hand, simply weighs more than what's recommended on the height/ weight tables."[4]

Often the height/weight charts used in approximating desired weight are erroneous or misleading. These charts overlook the importance of percentage of fat in proper determination of ideal weight. (Percent of fat is determined by the use of underwater weighing equipment and skin-fold calipers). The ideal percentage of body fat for males is around 12 percent (youth) and 15 percent (adult). For females, it's around 19 percent (youth and adult). The upper limits are 20 percent for a young boy or man, 25 percent for a young girl, and 30 percent for an adult woman. When the percentage of body fat is greater, the person is considered obese, even though the charts indicate that his or her weight is in line with what is "normal."

The best activities for weight control are those already listed as contributing to cardiovascular endurance.

Fitness: The Key To Joyful Living

DYNAMIC fitness is high on the list of prerequisites for health and well-being. There are other important factors — selection of nutritious foods, for example. The body needs good fuel and must be protected from substances that damage and waste its resources. You also need adequate rest, regular physical examinations, appropriate medical care, and good relaxation habits. These factors and others should be combined for a program of overall fitness that will help prevent disease, improve the functioning of your body systems, increase efficiency, and perhaps even lengthen your life expectancy.

Most of us have had the experience of beginning an exercise session feeling run-down and tired and then feeling pleasantly tired but somehow uplifted after the exercise. Whether this better feeling is the result of physiological and psychological changes or a sense of worth because of accomplishing a task and disciplining oneself has not been determined. But it is apparent that people on exercise programs have more pep, vigor, and enthusiasm.[5] Some call it a better outlook on life. Others say they feel better, are more confident, and face the problems of living in a more relaxed manner. They learn to lose themselves in play activities and relax, to experience a "joy of living"; this is perhaps the most important product of fitness.

1. The President's Council on Physical Fitness and Sports, *Physical Fitness Digest,* 1:1971, p. 1.
2. G.A. Sheehan, *Dr. Sheehan on Running.* Mountain View, CA: World Publications, 1975, p. 127.
3. C.T. Kuntzleman, "Can You Pass This Fitness Test?" *Fitness For Living,* January/February, 1972, p. 33.
4. C.T. Kuntzleman, *Activetics.* NY: Peter H. Wyden, 1975, p. 47.
5. F. Heinzleman and R.W. Bagley, "Response to Physical Activity Programs and Their Effect on Health Behavior," *Public Health Reports,* 85:1970, p. 905.

Glossary

Abduction: Moving a limb away from the midline of the body. The term also refers to an exercise which does the same. Abductor muscles are involved.

Achilles Tendon: The strong tendon that attaches the large calf muscles to the heel bone.

Adaptation: One of the physiological principles of physical training. If the body is subjected to physical stress (as in the training techniques required by lifting and running), it will usually adapt to that stress. If the stress is increased, the body will soon be able to work harder and with less fatigue.

Adduction: Moving a limb toward the midline of the body. The term also refers to an exercise which does the same. Adductor muscles are involved.

Adductor Magnus: Powerful triangular muscle in the inner thigh. It draws the leg toward the body.

Aorta: The largest artery of the body. It distributes purified blood to all parts of the body.

Athlete's Heart: An enlarged heart attained as a result of endurance type physical exercise over an extended period of time. It is not the same as the pathologically enlarged heart that occurs in some kinds of heart disease. The increase in size due to exercise generally indicates a more efficient heart, one which pumps up twice as much blood per beat as an untrained heart.

Barbell: A long iron bar to which iron plates can be or are attached.

Biceps Brachii: Muscles at the front of the upper arms that bend the elbows and make it possible to bring objects toward your body.

Dumbbell: A short iron bar to which iron plates can be or are attached.

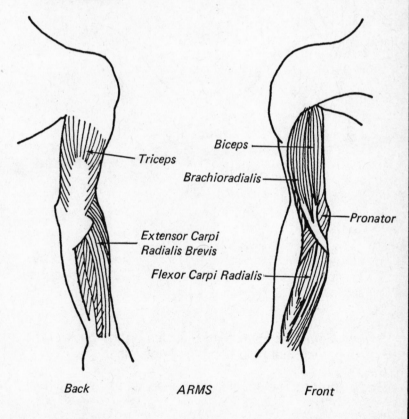

Triceps

Biceps

Brachioradialis

Pronator

Extensor Carpi
Radialis Brevis

Flexor Carpi Radialis

Back   *ARMS*   Front

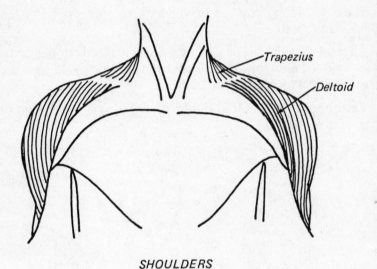

Trapezius

Deltoid

SHOULDERS

View

Biceps Femoris: Hamstring muscles on the back of the upper leg that help bend the knee joint.

Body Toning: The conditioning, shaping, and strengthening of the body through weight-training exercises.

Brachioradialis: Muscle of the top forearm. You can feel it contract and relax when you wiggle your fingers or do exercises such as the wrist curl.

Carbon Dioxide: One of the major constituents of exhaled air. Carbon dioxide is also found in fatigued muscles.

Cardiovascular System: The circulatory and respiratory systems — heart, arteries, capillaries, veins, lungs, and lymph ducts — that provide the body cells with blood-supplying oxygen and nutrients and that carry off wastes.

Carpus (or Carpal Bones): The wrist bones.

Cartilage: Tough, fibrous tissue that forms cushions between bones and protects them from shock. In joints, the cartilage cells are enclosed in capsules. Great pain results when these capsules become dry or are ruptured.

Cervical Vertebrae: Vertebrae of the backbone from the shoulders to the base of the brain. Because they are less well-supported than the lower vertebrae, cervical vertebrae are particularly susceptible to injury from impact.

Clavicle: The collar bone, running from the shoulder to the breast bone, or sternum. It is one of the most easily broken bones.

Coccyx: The tail bone.

Deltoid: Cap-like muscle over each shoulder. These bulging muscles raise the arms.

Diathermy: Therapeutic application of heat, usually in the form of heat pads, hot water bottles, heat lamps, or hot compresses.

Dumbbell

Barbell

Dual-Resistance Exercises: Exercises in which one person strains against resistance offered by another person. The partner acts as a weight to be lifted, moved, or resisted as the other person pushes or pulls. If there is body movement, the exercises are isotonic. If no movement occurs, they are isometric. Dual-resistance exercises, which require no equipment and little space, develop muscle strength and endurance and can readily be adapted to improve specific areas of the body.

Dumbbell: A short iron bar to which iron plates can be or are attached.

Extensors: Muscles which make possible the extending of a joint.

External Oblique: Muscles at the side of the torso.

Femur: The thigh bone.

Fibula: The smaller of the two bones of the lower leg. The thicker one is the tibia.

Flexor: Muscles whose contractions bend hinge joints (such as the elbows and knees).

Gastrocnemius: The largest muscle in the calf of the leg. It extends the foot, raises the heel, and assists in bending the knee.

Gluteus Maximus: The broad, thick, rounded muscle near the surface of the buttocks.

Humerus: The bone of the upper arm.

Iliotibial Band: The band of muscles extending along the outer thigh from the hip to the knee.

Ilium: The large, thin, wing-shaped hip bones protecting the pelvic area on either side.

Lactic Acid: A colorless, syrupy acid that is a waste product of sugar oxidation. It is found in muscle tissue after exercise and causes a feeling of fatigue.

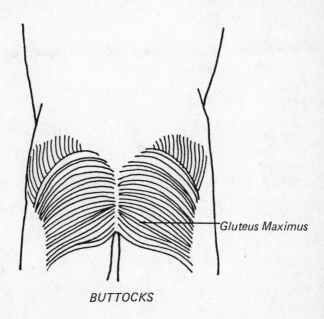

Gluteus Maximus

BUTTOCKS

Latissimus Dorsi ("lats"): A broad, flat muscle on each side of the lower part of the back. The muscle draws the arm backward and downward and rotates the front of the arm toward the body.

Ligament: Tissue that fastens bones together and holds organs in place. Ligaments may appear as cords, bands, or sheets. A sprain occurs when ligaments covering a joint are twisted or torn.

Lumbar Vertebrae: Vertebrae of the backbone from the waist to the sacrum.

Muscle-bound: Having enlarged muscles which have lost some of their flexibility.

Muscle Endurance: The ability to perform repeated muscle movements.

Muscle Strength: The ability to exert force against resistance.

Muscular Power: The ability to exert force against resistance quickly.

Overhand Grip: Grasping the bar, barbell or dumbbell with palms facing down.

Patella: The knee cap.

Pectorals (or Pectoralis Major): The muscles that lie beneath the breast or the top of the chest.

Phalanges: The fourteen bones of the fingers and toes.

Pronator: Muscles of the forearm which enable you to turn the hand palm inward.

Prone: Lying on your stomach.

Pulse Rate: The rate at which the heart beats. The normal

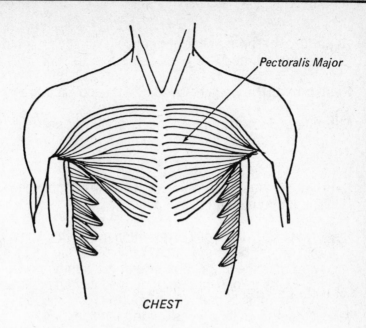

Pectoralis Major

CHEST

pulse rate for adults ranges from 66 to 85 beats per minute, although some people have lower or higher pulse rates with no discernible ill effects. Athletes often lower their resting pulse rates into the 50s. Strenuous exercise may temporarily increase the pulse rate by 40 to 100 beats per minute or more.

Radius: The larger of the two bones of the forearm. The other bone is the ulna.

Range Of Motion: The distance through which a limb can travel at a particular joint.

Recovery Time: The time between sets.

Rectus Abdominis: The broad, flat muscles of the abdomen.

Rectus Femoris: The straight muscle of the femur, or thigh bone, located at the front of the hip. It aids in walking and running.

Repetitions: The number of complete muscular contractions performed in a particular exercise.

Resistance: The weight moved by a muscular contraction.

Sacroiliac: The joint that connects the backbone with the pelvis. Strain in the sacroiliac may cause lower back ache.

Sacrum: Five fused vertebrae of the vertebral column. The sacrum forms part of the pelvis.

Sartorius: The long, flat, narrow thigh muscle that helps to lift the leg, bend the knee, and rotate the thigh outward. It is the longest muscle in the human body. It's called the tailor's muscle. It derived its name because it is the muscle that allows you to cross one leg over another to sit in a cross-legged fashion.

Scapula: The shoulder blade. The scapula contains a shallow depression into which the round head of the humerus fits to form the shoulder ball-and-socket joint. The shoulder joint can move in any direction, but it is also easily dislocated.

Set: A given number of repetitions.

Soleus: A broad, flat muscle in the calf. It lies underneath the gastrocnemius muscle.

Sternocleidomastoid: A muscle on each side of the neck. It tenses when the head is turned. It attaches to the breast bone and just below the ear.

Sternum: The middle bone in the front of the chest. The upper ribs are attached to this bony shield, which is also called the breastbone. The diaphragm is attached at the bottom of the sternum.

Supinator: Muscles of the forearm which enable you to turn your hand palm upward.

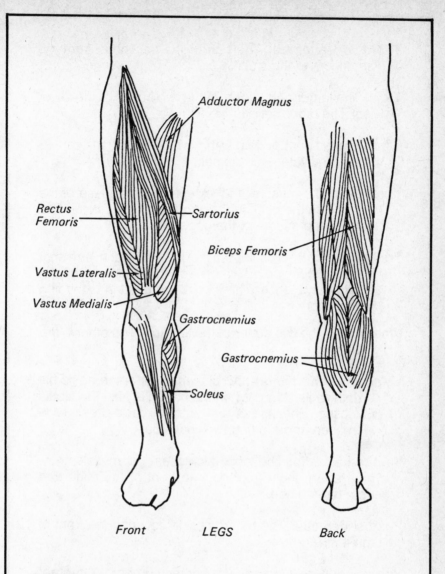

Adductor Magnus

Rectus
Femoris

Sartorius

Biceps Femoris

Vastus Lateralis

Vastus Medialis

Gastrocnemius

Gastrocnemius

Soleus

Front   LEGS   Back

Supine: Lying on your back.

Tendon: Tough white fibers twisted spirally into a cord that
moves bones by pulling on muscles. The tendon
slides up and down inside a sheath, like an arm in a
shirt sleeve. When there has been undue stress on
the tendon, the sheath can become inflamed. A torn or
cut tendon can be sewn together and will usually heal.

Thoracic Vertebrae: The part of the backbone from the shoulders to the waist.

Tibia: The larger and thicker of the two bones of the lower leg. The other bone is the fibula.

Time: The amount of time within which repetitions can be done; equivalent to one set.

Trapezius: The muscles that extend from the base of the skull down the neck to the shoulders. They come to a point in the middle of the upper back.

Triceps Brachii: Muscles at the back of each arm that become contracted when you hold your arm out straight and tense. The triceps are used in extending your arms.

Ulna: One of the two bones of the forearm. The other is the radius.

Valsava Phenomenon: Occurs when a person holds his breath while lifting. When the breath is held the glottis is closed. Because of that, intra-thoracic pressure is increased and a person will pass out.

Vastus Lateralis: The long, thick sheath of muscles running at an angle from back to front of the thigh and from hip to knee.

Vastus Medialis: The broad muscle covering the front of the thigh.

Vertebrae: See Cervical Vertebrae; Lumbar Vertebrae; Thoracic Vertebrae.

Weighted Boot: A heavier shoe that can accommodate additional weights.

Index

Trainer-Matic, 221-22
triceps
    rope exercises for, 169
    warm up exercises for, 132
    weight training exercises for, 73,
      153
    see also arm muscles
trunk twist, 121

V

varicose veins, 17
V-sit-up, 183

W

walking squat, 92-93
warming up, 119-20
    calisthenics for, 120-43
    weight workouts for, 144
waist muscles
    exercises for, 124, 140
    see also abdominal muscles
weight control, 11-13
Weight Machine, 218-19
weight training
    benefits of, 16-17
    and body tone, 10
    calisthenics to prepare for, 31-45

CONSUMER GUIDE® program for,
    100-17
    danger signals with, 55-56
    effects on females of, 6, 8
    health requirements for, 19-20
    myths associated with, 8-9
    rules for, 56-57, 190
    with a partner, 174-88
    principles of, 48-54
    safety checklist for, 101, 190-92
    as a sport, 8-9
    and sports performance, 6-7,
      112-16
    and weight control, 11-13, 17
weight training equipment. *See*
    equipment for weight training
weight training facilities. *See* facilities
    for weight training
wrist abduction, 80
wrist adduction, 81
wrist curl, 74
wrist extensor, 76-77
wrist roller, 82
wrist sprains, 202

Y

YMCA Sit-Up Test, 31